Sixteen
And Away

ARLETA RICHARDSON

Chariot Books
DAVID C. COOK PUBLISHING CO.

*To Margaret
who shared a grandmother
with me*

Chariot Books is an imprint of the David C. Cook Publishing Co.
David C. Cook Publishing Co., Elgin, Illinois 60120
David C. Cook Publishing Co., Weston, Ontario

SIXTEEN AND AWAY FROM HOME
© 1985 by Arleta Richardson

Cover illustration by Dora Leder

First printing, 1985
Printed in the United States of America
89 88 87   5 4

Library of Congress Cataloging in Publication Data

Richardson, Arleta.
  Sixteen and away from home.

  Summary: In 1889 two sixteen-year-olds leave their homes to go to the academy in town, where they stay with relatives and enjoy being "grown up."
  1. Children's stories, American. [1. Schools—Fiction. 2. Friendship—Fiction] I. Title.
PZ7.R3942Si 1985   [Fic]   85-438
ISBN 0-89191-933-3

Contents

1 The Last Free Summer 5

2 Time to Leave Home 16

3 School Begins 27

4 The Honor System 37

5 The Most Popular Boy in School 47

6 Thomas Gives a Party 58

7 A Thump on the Head 68

8 A Honey of an Idea 77

9 An Error in Judgment 88

10 Coals of Fire 97

11 An Unwelcome Guest 106

12 Hearts and Arrows 119

13 Mrs. Owens Has Her Say 129

14 The Most Important Event 139

15 A Friend Is Forever 151

1
The Last
Free Summer

FOR MY BIRTHDAY MA BOUGHT ME A journal. In it I am supposed to record the most important moments of my life. She wrote in the front:

The journal of Mabel Jessica O'Dell, started on her sixteenth birthday, June 23, 1889.

I showed it to Sarah Jane Clark, my best friend. "The problem," I explained, "is that I'm not always sure which are significant events and which will turn out to be everyday things. How does one know what is momentous?"

"When you're sixteen, *everything* is momentous, Mabel," she told me. "We've finished district school, and in the fall we'll be starting our final two years at the academy. Isn't that momentous enough for you?"

I watched Sarah Jane chew a piece of grass. Her face was calm and uncreased by worry. I wished I could face life as nonchalantly as she did.

"We haven't heard the results of our entrance examinations yet," I reminded her. "They were *not* easy, in spite of the hours we spent studying with Mrs. Porter. The academy could still turn us down, you know."

"I haven't come this far in life to be turned down for *anything*, Mabel. Of course they'll take us. They took Warren Carter, didn't they?"

I chose not to answer. Sarah Jane knew it required all my efforts to stay ahead of Warren in everything, and in math I usually couldn't. Though Warren was a year older than we were, and had passed his entrance exams for the academy a year earlier, he had stayed out a year to help his pa and save money for school. We'd be starting in the same class in the fall, and I knew Warren would still rather die than let a girl beat him.

I flipped through the blank pages of my journal. "I wish I knew now what will fill these, so I could prepare for it. I don't feel as ready to leave home as I thought I would."

"You're only going to be an hour away by train, for goodness' sake," scoffed Sarah Jane. "You'll be so busy you won't have time to think about it. Besides, you'll have me. Haven't we always gone through everything together?"

I nodded. "I think it's wonderful that your

aunt and uncle are going to let us stay with them. They're probably lonesome now that your cousin Laura is married."

"Mabel, do you really suppose we're old enough not to get homesick?"

Secretly I had my doubts, but I wasn't about to admit it to Sarah Jane. "You said yourself that we'd be too busy."

We got up from under the tree and started slowly down the lane. "It's almost time for Pa to be back with the mail. Maybe the letter will come today. Oh, Sarah Jane! I don't think I could stand it if we weren't accepted!"

"Where's your faith, Mabel? The Bible says wait patiently for the Lord, and he'll give you the desires of your heart. Of course," she added, "patient waiting has never been your strong point. I suppose that could nullify the promise."

She grinned and dodged as I swung at her.

"Do you think your ma is going to let you wear long skirts and put your hair up?"

I looked down at my dress, which almost reached the top of my high shoes. "I don't think she'll allow much longer than this," I replied. "She doesn't like to see young girls looking like grown women. And I'm sure I won't be allowed to put my hair up."

I'd done my best to persuade Ma that a girl in high school should look more adult.

"You'll look grown-up enough with your hair pulled back in a ribbon," she had decreed. "You have three-fourths of your life to pin your hair on top of your head."

"I can't put my hair up, either," Sarah Jane said. "Do you ever suspect that our mothers meet at night after we're in bed and decide what we're not going to be able to do next?"

There was no chance to answer, because Pa turned into the lane just at that moment. When he saw us, he waved a white envelope in the air.

"It's come! I can't look, Sarah Jane. I'll never be able to open it!"

Pa stopped beside us and handed me the envelope. I stood holding it in shaking hands while Sarah Jane danced around me.

"Mabel, if you don't get that letter out of there this very second, I'm going to pound you! What are you waiting for?"

It doesn't seem that one's whole future could be decided in a split second, but I felt that mine would be. My heart beat wildly as I pulled the letter out and read it.

This is to confirm that Mabel J. O'Dell has passed the entrance examinations with high honors. Her application to enter Rosemond Academy in September, 1889, has been approved.

I grabbed Sarah Jane and hugged her. Then I grabbed Pa's leg, which was all I could reach, and hugged him, too.

"Mine must be here, too," Sarah Jane exclaimed. "I've got to run. Come over after dinner." She was gone.

I raced for the house. "It came!" I called. "I passed! I've been accepted at the academy."

Ma held the screen door open for me, which was a good thing—I probably would have gone right through it.

"Can you believe it, Ma? Can you really believe it?"

"Why, Mabel, I didn't expect anything else. I'm very pleased for you. Now if you can come down to earth long enough to help me get dinner on the table. . . ." But I had already started for the door.

"Where are you going?" she called.

"To see what Sarah Jane's letter says, of course. We need to talk about getting ready."

"You'll eat your dinner first," Ma said firmly. "You have two months to talk. We'll both go over to the Clarks' this afternoon. The plans must be discussed with her folks, too, you know."

It was hard to sit down and eat.

"Just think," I sighed happily, "I have a whole new life ahead of me. Who knows what marvelous things may happen?"

"There was a time when just the thought of the things that might happen could turn my hair," Ma declared. "I'm not all that restful yet about the two of you going off together."

"Why, Ma! We're young ladies now. We won't be doing foolish things. What could possibly go wrong?"

Ma sighed and eyed me thoughtfully. "You *look* like young ladies," she admitted. "But longer skirts and pulled-back hair are not positive proofs of maturity. Didn't I see you jump the fence the other evening?"

Pa snickered, and I blushed. "Probably. I have to be sure I can still do it. But that doesn't mean that I'm not grown-up. I am!"

"I hope so," Ma said. "I certainly hope so."

Sarah Jane met us at her porch, and the look on her face caused my heart to drop down to my toes. She said hello and held the door open for Ma to go into the house.

"What's the matter?" I demanded. "Didn't they accept you?"

"I'm accepted," Sarah Jane replied. "But Ma had a letter from Aunt Rhoda. She and Uncle Bert are going to be gone for several weeks on business. And they'll leave before school starts!"

"You mean we won't have a place to live? Oh, how terrible! My ma and pa would never allow me to go live in town with strangers."

"Mine either. There's only one hope. Aunt Rhoda says the housekeeper is very reliable and will be able to look after things until they return. She wants us to come right ahead as planned. Ma says they'll talk it over with your folks. Do you suppose they'll think we're responsible enough to be trusted?"

I stared bleakly at Sarah Jane. "If they base their judgment solely on past performance, we're doomed."

She sighed. "I know. I wish we hadn't done anything stupid since we were little kids, but you've had some pretty awful ideas."

"*I* have! You've gotten us into far more trouble than I ever have!"

Sarah Jane started to protest, and then she burst out laughing. "You know we could never prove that one way or the other, Mabel. If anything went wrong, we were both in it."

"Well, anyway, that's all in the past," I declared. "The Bible says, 'forgetting those things which are behind, and reaching forth unto those things which are before. . . .' We'll make up our minds to be serious students and prove what we can do."

We sat silently for a moment. "Are you praying, Mabel?" Sarah Jane asked. "If we ever needed to pray, this is the time."

"Yes, I am. I don't believe the Lord would let us pass the exams and be accepted, and then snatch the opportunity away from us. Do you? What good could come from that?"

"None that *I* can see, but the Lord knows better than we do."

I was saved from commenting by Mrs. Clark and Ma coming out of the kitchen.

"We've decided that you may go," Mrs. Clark announced. "If you aren't old enough to look after yourselves by now, you never will be."

"Oh, thank you! Thank you!" Sarah Jane and I smothered them with hugs.

"We'll be so responsible that you won't even know us!" cried Sarah Jane. "How will we ever get through the next two months?"

"I'd suggest you use them to get clothes ready," her mother answered. "Eight weeks isn't very long to make new dresses and underthings. That should keep you both out of trouble."

Sarah Jane's mother was right. The next weeks were filled with buying material, stitching seams, and trying on new outfits.

"I've never had so many new things at one time," I told Ma as we sewed.

"You've never been away from home for a year," Ma replied. She looked at me critically. "I hope you've grown as tall as you're going to be. I used to put deep hems in your dresses when you were little, but they don't look appropriate now."

I dropped the nightgown I was stitching. "Oh, Ma. Do you really think I'm full grown? That scares me."

"Just because you've reached your full height doesn't mean you can't grow on the inside, Mabel. That's where it counts the most."

Ma bent over her sewing, and as I looked at her, I thought how much I'd miss her. Maybe I wasn't ready to leave home yet.

"You didn't add 'and goodness knows you need to grow some,' " I told her. "Do you really think I'll get along all right without you?"

"Why, of course you will. We've brought you up to know right from wrong and to trust the Lord for your future. Pa and I rely on you to make the most of your high school years." Ma bit off a thread and laughed. Besides, when you two find out that whatever you get into you'll have to get out of on your own, it's bound to have a subduing effect on your actions!"

The days passed swiftly. As Mrs. Clark had predicted, we had no time for foolishness. Two days before we were to leave, we sat under our favorite tree at the end of the lane.

"Our childhood is behind us, Mabel," Sarah Jane said solemnly. "We are no longer young, innocent, and carefree. We probably won't have much opportunity to smile from now on."

"Sarah Jane! We're going to school, not to the penitentiary! Warren says it will be lots of fun."

"Warren Carter!" Sarah Jane sniffed. "He thinks the extraction of the biquadrate root is fun."

"I'll admit he's not much given to frivolity," I said, "but I'm sure he has his lighter moments."

"Of course. Walking twice briskly around the school campus before breakfast every morning."

I couldn't deny that possibility, nor could I think of anything to brighten Sarah Jane's mood. Even the evening train whistle in the distance sounded dismal. Suddenly she flopped over on her stomach, and her shoulders began to shake.

"Sarah Jane, what's the matter? Are you crying?"

"No," she choked, "I'm just recalling some of *our* lighter moments. Remember the day Wesley Patterson ran me down on the school ground, and we fastened his suspenders to his desk chair? Oh, my. That was a terrible thing to do!"

She hooted again, and I joined her. By the time we had wiped the tears from our faces, we were positive that the next two years of school held the possibility for as much pleasure as our past ten years had given. We couldn't wait to begin.

2

Time to Leave Home

SEPTEMBER 2, 1889. Ma and I finished packing my trunk tonight, and I should be in bed, but I'm too excited to sleep. Tomorrow is the beginning of a great adventure. I want to be a good and sensible student, although I'll probably have to settle for good—Ma says I've never been terribly sensible. Pa prayed for us tonight, and it's comforting to know that the Lord is going to school with us tomorrow.

I WAS AWAKE BEFORE DAYLIGHT. WHEN PA left for the barn, I got up and dressed.

"There's something sad about doing anything for the last time, isn't there, Ma?" I said as we got breakfast. "I won't be making my bed here again until Christmas."

"You won't be spilling sugar on my floor again, either," Ma replied. "I can't say that I see a great deal of sadness in that."

I went to get the broom. "You know what I mean. Things are going to be different."

"Yes, I know. We're going to miss you, Mabel, even though I do complain about your carelessness. But I'm glad you have the chance to go to school. If you do well, you may have a school of your own in another two years."

I contemplated that in silence. A school of my own! Could I really learn enough to do that? Mrs. Porter thought I could, and so did Ma and Pa. I determined that I would not disappoint them.

Pa took us to the train. Just before we reached the Clarks' place, I asked him to stop.

"Pa, you won't forget how much I love you and Ma, will you?"

He hugged me tight. "Of course not," he said huskily. "You're still our little girl, even if you are a young lady. We'll pray for you every day, and Christmas will be here before you know it."

The excitement of seeing our trunks put on the train and finding our seats carried us through the first few minutes. But when the train began to move, and Pa and Mr. Clark faded from view, we looked at each other with apprehension.

"I hope you brought your journal with you, Mabel," said Sarah Jane. "I have a feeling you're going to have a lot to say."

At the end of our hour's ride, we found no one waiting for us at the train station.

"This is not a propitious beginning," Sarah Jane moaned. "Do you think Aunt Rhoda forgot we were coming today, and the housekeeper doesn't know?"

"I suppose that's possible," I said. "There's nothing we can do but wait. We couldn't carry our trunks even if we knew the way."

We sat down on a bench near the depot. Crowds of people passed by, but no one appeared to be looking for two girls.

"I'm thinking about panicking," Sarah Jane said. "How long have we been here?"

I consulted the big clock over the station. "At least five minutes."

"Miss Sarah Jane and Miss Mabel?" said a voice beside us. "I'm Jacob. If you'd like to get into the buggy, I'll bring your trunks."

We climbed in, and the buggy was soon headed down the tree-lined street. We looked about eagerly to see how much we remembered from the week-long visit we had made years before.

"The town doesn't look as big as it used to, does it?" I whispered. "How could something shrink so much in eight years?"

"We've grown, Mabel. Things always look big when you're little. The house will be the same."

It was. The big three-story house with the spiked fence around it was familiar. But it was not Sarah Jane's cousin Laura who opened the door.

"Lettie, here are the young ladies who will be staying with us," said Jacob. "If you want to take them upstairs, I'll bring the trunks."

The housekeeper's head bent ever so slightly in our direction. "Of course. This way, please."

Silently she led the way up the broad staircase and down the corridor. When she stopped abruptly in front of the closed door, I barely missed colliding with her. Sarah Jane, following close behind, banged into me sharply.

Lettie opened the door. "This is your room. The bathroom is across the hall." She surveyed us coldly. "I will change your towels three times a week and your bed linen weekly. You are responsible for your own room; I will clean the bathroom. I do not fetch and carry for able-bodied young ladies. The midday meal is served promptly at twelve-fifteen. Please be on time."

She spun around and descended the stairs, leaving us gaping after her in astonishment.

"I knew we'd have a housekeeper looking after us, but I had no idea she'd be so . . ."

"Awesome," Sarah Jane finished for me. "I don't remember running into her when we were here before, but Aunt Rhoda says she's been with them forever. Do you suppose she'll get used to us?"

"I expect so. Ma says a person can get used to anything if he has to."

We walked around our room, peering into the closet and dresser drawers. Aunt Rhoda had furnished the room with a big four-poster bed, a bookcase, a rocker, and two desks. The window looked out over the backyard, and we could see the big barn.

"Remember how disappointed we were when we learned there weren't any cows or chickens in that barn?" I said with a laugh.

"Yes, and how we didn't dare go outside that fence for fear we'd get lost. And here we are grown-up and on our own—almost."

We sat down on the bed. "I don't think she likes us much," Sarah Jane added.

I knew the "she" referred to Lettie.

"I wonder why?" Sarah Jane continued. "Aunt Rhoda must have talked it over with her before we came. She may be a good housekeeper, but she's so imposing."

I agreed. "Maybe she's not used to having girls underfoot anymore."

"This is one girl who won't be under her foot," Sarah Jane stated grimly. "Believe me, I'll give her all the room she needs."

At that moment Jacob appeared in the doorway with my trunk. "Here you are, young lady. I'll be right back with the other one." He turned and looked at us kindly. "She's a hard one, is Lettie, but she's fair. You'll get used to her ways."

"A friend amongst the Philistines," I said after Jacob disappeared. "I'm glad he lives here, too."

A clock struck in the lower regions of the house, and we jumped up quickly.

"We'd better wash up and straighten our hair," Sarah Jane gasped. "It won't do to be late. She'd probably take all the food back to the kitchen by twelve-sixteen if we weren't there."

The table was set with just two plates, and we took our places silently. Lettie put the food before us and disappeared.

"Aren't Lettie and Jacob going to eat with us?"

"They eat in the kitchen, I guess." Sarah Jane looked around the big dining room. "When you're used to eating with a family, this seems pretty bleak."

I nodded. "I suppose it wouldn't be a good thing to ask if we could eat in the kitchen with them, would it?"

We knew it wouldn't, so we said our own blessing and ate our meal. "Are we going to survive ten whole months of this?" Sarah Jane wondered.

"Yes, we are," I told her. "We came here to go to school because the Lord made a way for us. This is just one of the 'all things' that is going to work for our good—although I admit I don't quite see how."

"If you young ladies have finished, I would like to clear the table." The chilly voice of Lettie moved us quickly from our chairs.

"Can we help you with the dishes?" Sarah Jane asked.

"I do not require help," Lettie answered stiffly. "Young ladies of breeding do not work in the kitchen."

We walked slowly out to the porch that surrounded the house on three sides. I started to sit down on the top step when Sarah Jane grabbed me.

"Young ladies of breeding do not sit on porch steps." She mimicked Lettie's tone so perfectly that I had to laugh.

"It's not funny, Mabel. She knows very well that we both grew up in a kitchen full of dishes to wash. For some reason she resents our being here."

"Why don't we go and look at the school, even if it isn't open yet?" I suggested. "We should find out where it is."

"We'll have to ask for directions, and I'm going to think several times before I bother Lettie. Let's see if we can find Jacob."

Jacob was in the barn, and he was glad to help. "Do you want to know the quick way to get there or the ladylike route?"

"Both," Sarah Jane answered. "What makes the fast way unladylike?"

Jacob's eyes twinkled. "I'll let you find that out. Follow that little path through the wooded area. When you come to a clearing, you're on the back of the school campus. If you want to come back the other way, follow the road in front of the classroom building east until you come to a fork. Take the left fork and it will bring you right back here."

The path through the woods was lovely and shady. "It looks well used. I can't see anything unladylike about it, can you?" I asked.

"Jacob must have been mistaken," Sarah Jane said. Then she stopped as we both spotted a fence.

"You might know the school would be surrounded by a fence," I said. "We can't step over *that*."

The split-rail fence was waist high. In order to get to the other side, it would be necessary to lift our skirts at least to our knees.

"We've never let that stop us before," Sarah Jane decided, and in a moment she was on the other side. I followed quickly, but

23

not before I had looked around carefully to see that no one was in sight.

"That isn't exactly the most graceful thing a lady can do," I said. "I suppose once we're through school we won't be able to jump fences any longer."

"I don't want to think about it," Sarah Jane said. "Let's go look at the school."

We stood and gazed at the three-storied building in silence. There appeared to be no one around, but the big front doors were open and we went in.

"I never thought I'd be going to a school I could get lost in," I said. "How many rooms do you suppose it has?"

"There are six on this floor," Sarah Jane counted. "So there are probably twelve more above us. If we have a different room for every class, that's going to take some getting used to."

"Good afternoon, young ladies. Were you looking for someone?"

We whirled around to see a tall, stately gentleman in a frock coat.

"No, sir," I stammered. "We were just looking at the building."

"Very well." He turned and disappeared into the room behind him. We scuttled out the front entrance and across the campus.

"Is there anyone in this town who doesn't

look as though he might break if he bent over?" Sarah Jane wanted to know. "Is perfect posture something we have to know to get out of school?"

"If it is, I hope the icy voice doesn't go with it," I declared. "I wonder who he is?"

"We'll ask Jacob. Let's go unpack our trunks while we still want to stay," she suggested. "Maybe we'll feel more at home."

Jacob was glad to fill us in. "That would be Mr. Kingman, the principal. He also teaches history, so you'll be seeing more of him."

I wasn't sure whether that was something to look forward to or not.

"Are you getting tired of being called a young lady?" I asked Sarah Jane as we put our things away.

She nodded. "I thought not being a child any longer was a good idea. Now I'm ready to change my mind."

As we got ready for bed, she brought up a subject I had been thinking about. "You know, Mabel, I've never gone to bed without having prayers. What are we going to do without our folks to pray with us?"

Suddenly the picture of Pa taking the Bible from the top of the china cupboard was so vivid that I felt terribly homesick.

"Well, there isn't any reason why we can't have our own," I decided. "We can take turns reading, Sarah Jane, and we both know how to pray."

When we had finished, I felt comforted and better able to face what lay ahead. But I might not have fallen asleep so peacefully had I known what the next day would bring.

3
School
Begins!

SEPTEMBER 3, 1889. The first day of school is behind us. I've been in school most of my life but I've never had a day like this. To begin with, S.J. and I are on opposite sides of the room in every class because we are seated alphabetically. This is the first time in our lives we have not shared a desk! Then, aside from Warren Carter, we didn't know another living soul.

I HADN'T THOUGHT ABOUT THERE BEING so many new people to meet, had you, Mabel?"

"No, but we should have. Students come from all over the state to attend here."

We were standing alone in a corner of the big assembly room. Boys and girls milled about us, shouting greetings to friends and laughing together.

"I feel like the only person in the world who doesn't know anyone," Sarah Jane said. "And I don't see any people who look as if they want to know me."

"We just walked in this minute," I reminded her. "We'll find out who the others are, and then we'll have friends."

I didn't feel as optimistic as I sounded. To come from a school where I'd been known since before the beginners class and be plopped down in the middle of a group who'd never heard of me before was unsettling, to say the least.

There was a sudden silence as Mr. Kingman entered the room and walked to the front. "Will you be seated, please," he instructed. "Young men on the left and young ladies on the right."

"He doesn't waste any time separating the sheep from the goats," Sarah Jane whispered, and I giggled nervously. We found chairs together and bowed our heads as the principal opened the school with prayer. Then he introduced the faculty members one by one.

"Miss Baker is the girls' preceptress. She teaches grammar and rhetoric, physical culture for women, and drawing.

"Mr. Justin teaches Latin, French, and men's physical training.

"Mrs. Gates teaches calculus, trigonometry, and biology.

"And I will teach history and government," Mr. Kingman concluded. There was polite applause as he sat down and Miss Baker rose.

"The entering students will be divided into two classes," she announced. "Listen carefully for your name; then report to the designated room where you will receive a copy of the school rules and your study schedule." She began to read, and Sarah Jane clutched my arm tightly. "What will we do if she puts us in different classes?" she moaned. "We'll never see each other again."

"That would be quite a feat, since we live in the same house," I answered. "Listen, or we'll miss our names."

Carter and Clark were read for the first class, and it seemed like a lifetime until I heard O'Dell and could breathe again. Our class was directed to go to Room 206 to meet with Mrs. Gates.

"Wouldn't you know I'd have to be in a class with the math teacher?" Sarah Jane said as we walked upstairs. "Besides taking calculus from her, I have to spend my study periods there, too. Do you suppose they think I'll learn logarithms by osmosis?"

"If they do, they're certainly going to be disillusioned," said a voice we knew at once.

"Oh, Warren, it's you. You mean we came all this way to be in a class with you again?"

"It looks like it." He turned to me. "I hope

29

you're prepared to be in second place this year. I've had twelve months to rest my brain, and I'm ready to show you how much smarter boys can be." He grinned cheerfully and walked to the room with us.

"I'm not going to concede before the first class," I replied haughtily. "Just don't plan on an easy victory."

We were assigned our seats, and monitors began to hand out class schedules. I looked around at my fellow students with interest, and a cheerful-looking girl across the aisle smiled at me. I started to speak to her when the girl behind me said loudly, "I don't know why they accept such hayseeds in this school, do you, Molly?"

I turned to see whom she was talking about, and found her staring at me.

Molly, the girl across the aisle, blushed and glared at her. "You should be ashamed of yourself, Clarice Owens! Is that any way to welcome a new student?"

Clarice shrugged, and Molly turned to me. "Don't worry about her; she doesn't always think before she opens her mouth. I'm Molly Matson, and I hope we'll be friends."

I was sure we would be, and I was equally sure that I would be avoiding Clarice as much as possible.

During the recess before our first class,

Sarah Jane and I compared class schedules.

1 Grammar and Rhetoric
2 Biology
3 Latin
4 Study
Noon
5 History
6 Calculus
7 Physical Culture for Women

"I guess everyone in this group has the same classes," Sarah Jane said. "That means we'll sit next to the same people all day long. At least I know Warren. Who sits by you?"

"Molly Matson is across the aisle and Clarice Owens is behind me," I told her. "I'd rather have Clarice in front of me where I could see her. I don't think I trust that one."

I was soon to discover that there was nothing underhanded about Clarice. She made sure I heard everything she said.

"Are you sure you can find all those places after being confined to one room for so many years?" she asked. Or, "I suppose you miss going for the cows before school in the morning."

"I can't even think of anything to say back," I sputtered to Sarah Jane. "Nothing comes to me until she's walked away."

"Maybe you should ask her what she has ,against hayseeds," Sarah Jane suggested. "I think she's just jealous because you're prettier than she is."

That wasn't true, but it was nice of Sarah Jane to say it.

Molly joined us as we left math class and headed for physical culture. Sarah Jane looked pale and shaken, and Molly commented on it.

"Anything that has to do with math makes her look like that," I said. "She'll come around."

"Thanks for your sympathy," Sarah Jane retorted. "You have no idea what tortures I suffer in there. How would you feel if you still had to add nine and six on your fingers?"

"Adding nine and anything is no trick," Molly said. "Just take one from the smaller number and make your nine ten. Then it's ten and whatever is left."

Sarah Jane stopped and looked at Molly with admiration. "Where were you when I was in the second grade?" she demanded. "And why didn't you ever tell me that, Mabel?"

"I didn't know you weren't already doing it," I replied. "Do you mean that you've been *counting* every number all this time?"

Sarah Jane nodded miserably. "And all these years I thought you were my best friend." She gave a sigh. "Little do we know the workings of another person's mind."

"Right," Molly laughed. "And now that you've found out you can't read each other's thoughts, let's enjoy the one hour of the day when we can move around and relax."

Miss Baker clapped her hands for attention. Then she announced, "We will have a very short class today to get organized. Each new girl will be given a pattern, and everyone will be expected to be in uniform by next Monday. The middy will be white cotton and the bloomers black sateen. Are there any questions?"

I stole a glance at Sarah Jane and was not surprised to see that she looked as dumbfounded as I felt. Miss Baker was still talking. "That will be all for today. Pick up your patterns on the way out."

"*Bloomers*?" Sarah Jane shrieked when we were outside. "Nothing but a waist on top of them? No skirt?"

"That's what we always wear for physical culture," Molly told her. "They're much easier to run and play games in than a skirt."

"But in *public?* Pa would send me to my room for a week if he saw me! In fact, he wouldn't let me *out* of my room like that in the first place!"

"We aren't actually in public," Molly said. "We stay in the lot behind the classroom building. No one thinks anything of it."

"That's one thing I won't tell Ma about," I declared. "I'm not sure she's ready to understand."

"Miss Baker is a firm believer in exercise for young ladies," Molly explained, "and she thinks skirts flying around are not modest."

"She's probably right," Sarah Jane agreed, "but I'm going to have a hard time feeling modest wearing my inside clothes on the outside!"

"It always takes a while for country girls to get used to city ways, but I'm sure you'll manage."

We had not heard Clarice come up beside us. She stopped and looked us over carefully. "I'd know you were from the farm, even if I hadn't heard you talking. What does it feel like to move into the world?"

"Clarice! Mabel and Sarah Jane passed the same exams you did to come here. You've no call to make rude remarks." Molly was indignant.

Clarice's eyes widened innocently. "I didn't say anything about their intelligence! How could you think I'd be so rude? It must be *lots* of fun to live on a farm, isn't it?" She smiled sweetly at us and walked away.

"I don't know what's the matter with her," Molly declared. "I've been in school with her since first grade, and though she's always thought she was better than the rest of us, I've never heard her be downright insulting before."

"Pa says everyone has a reason for being the way he is," I said. "If we can find out what her reason is, we might be able to help her get over it."

"I'd like to smack her first, and then find out her reasons," Sarah Jane exclaimed. "And don't tell me that's not the Christian attitude, because I already know it. I just wish the Lord would avenge his children more speedily."

"Don't worry about it," Molly said. "Come on home with me. Mama will help you with your uniforms, and if we're lucky there will be lemonade and cookies."

Mrs. Matson was glad to help us. "We can whip these up in no time," she assured us. "Molly needs a new pair this year, too, and I'll make them all at once. Are there many new students in your section this year?"

"I guess about ten, Mama," Molly replied. "So many come from the districts for their last years that they need two sections of this class," she explained to us. "Some of us from town have been in the high school since our ninth year, but we have new students each fall. I'm glad you two are in my section. I just know we're going to have fun together!"

"I wish everyone in the class welcomed us as much as Molly does," I said to Sarah Jane on the way home, "but I know we need to give it time."

I was almost asleep that night when Sarah Jane spoke. "Who does Clarice Owens remind me of? I'm sure it will come to me if I think hard enough."

"If it does, don't tell me," I answered. "I can't believe I've ever known anyone as hateful as she is."

"Mary Etta Rose Amanda Morgan!" Sarah Jane declared. "Except that her hair isn't red, Clarice could be Mary Morgan all over again. Don't you think so?"

"I told you not to tell me," I sighed. "Up till now I'd done a good job of forgetting Mary Morgan. But, yes, I guess you're right."

I knew I should pray for Clarice, but I fell asleep thinking it would take more than prayer to make her fit to live with.

4
The Honor System

October 10, 1889. We've been in school for over a month, and I'm beginning to feel as if I belong here. There are a lot of nice girls—and boys, too—in our class.

Awhile ago Mrs. Gates explained in chapel about the honor system. We have to sign our test papers to say that we have not given or received help. Also, we are obligated to tell if we see others breaking the rules. That is for the good of all, Mrs. Gates says. At the time, I hoped I would never see anything that needed reporting. . . .

"OH, BOTHER! I PICKED UP CLARICE'S Latin book instead of mine. Now she'll have something else to complain about."

Sarah Jane looked up from her desk. "I don't know what difference it makes—her book says the same thing yours does. Just take it back in the morning and tell her you took it by mistake."

"That's easy for you to say. She goes out of

her way to find things wrong with me. She'll enjoy having more ammunition." I pulled my notebook toward me. "But there's nothing I can do about it now. Do you have your translation done?"

"Nope," Sarah Jane replied. "I'm still on my math. Why do they give the answers to a problem and then make you tell how they got it?"

"To improve your analytical powers," I told her. "It's excellent discipline. You'll be a stronger person for it."

"Oh, be quiet and work on your Latin. And don't be so smug just because you were born knowing how to do algebra."

I laughed at her and opened the Latin book, then just as quickly slammed it shut.

"Did it bite you?" Sarah Jane inquired.

"She has the translations written in!"

Sarah Jane looked at me blankly. "Written in? You mean she wrote the English over the Latin, or the Latin over the English?"

"Both, I think." I opened the book again and quickly flipped the pages. "The whole *book* is translated! She hasn't learned all this yet. Someone else has done it."

"I never would have thought of something like that," Sarah Jane said. "I wonder where she got the translation?"

"Probably bought the book from a former

student, or had a relative in class. Anyway, I don't want it. Let me use your book until you finish your math." I pushed Clarice's book aside and began to work on my lesson.

"Mabel, aren't you honor bound to report her?"

"You mean tell Mr. Justin that Clarice cheated? I can't do that!" I wailed.

"You could certainly hold it over her head," Sarah Jane replied. "If she knows you have something you *could* tell, it might make a difference in her attitude."

"She'll know, all right, when I take her book back tomorrow. But I'm pretty sure it won't make her my everloving friend. She'll just be mad at me for finding out."

It took me nearly an hour to do three pages of translation. Between listening to Sarah Jane mutter over her math and struggling with my conscience over what to do about Clarice, it was hard to keep my mind on the genitive, ablative, and accusative cases.

The first person I saw the next morning was Clarice. She wasn't furious, as I had expected her to be. Instead she gave me an unpleasant smile.

"That was certainly a stupid thing you did, to pick up my Latin book last night. I suppose you know it's your Christian duty to report me." She looked at me triumphantly.

"But how are you going to prove to Mr. Justin that you didn't copy all the lessons while you had it? Besides, I can always swear that the translations weren't there before you took it. He'll believe me!" She smirked again and flounced off, leaving me staring after her in disbelief.

"That's exactly what she'd do, too," I moaned to Molly and Sarah Jane. "Now what happens?"

"As I see it, you're between a rock and a hard place," Sarah Jane decided after thinking it over. "You're in trouble if you don't tell, and you're in trouble if you do."

"I've figured that out by myself," I snapped. "I need a solution, not a diagnosis."

"It might do some good to remember that the Bible says the wrongdoer will always suffer for his sin," Molly suggested hopefully.

"I'm not nearly as anxious to see Clarice suffer as I am to keep myself from suffering," I replied. "It's my word against hers. What if Mr. Justin decides he has no choice but to fail us both?"

"He couldn't do that!" Sarah Jane looked stricken.

"He could," Molly said with a nod. "Both the one who receives help and the one who gives it are subject to discipline. That's how the honor system works. However," she added, "I don't think he would fail you. He might just lower your grade."

Visions of Warren Carter crowing over his higher grade average floated before me, and I groaned. "Now I know how Job felt when his comforters gathered around him," I declared. "You two are less than no help at all. I guess it's my problem, but I don't think it's right to tell on someone else."

" 'Work out your own salvation with fear and trembling,' " Sarah Jane quoted. "You shouldn't have any trouble with the fear and trembling part, anyway."

"Sometimes your aptness with biblical admonitions is a bit irritating," I told her. "Couldn't you just say you're sorry for me once in a while?"

"Oh, I am, Mabel! I really am. It's just that you seldom have any trouble that I haven't gotten you into. I don't know how to handle it." Sarah Jane looked so unhappy that I couldn't be angry with her. After all, there wasn't much she could do.

In history class we were studying the Revolutionary War period. My mind wasn't really on the lecture until Mr. Kingman asked a question. "When an individual, or group of individuals, feels that a law is unfair, what should they do about it? What would you have done if you had been among those in Boston who refused to pay tax to England?"

"You can't break a law just because you don't like it," Warren said. "That would be anarchy."

"That's exactly what they had," Mr. Kingman replied. "What would be a reasonable alternative?"

"You could find all the people who feel the same way you do and change the law," suggested Thomas Charles.

Several more ideas were added, but I had stopped listening. I couldn't wait until class was over to share my thought with Molly and Sarah Jane.

"That's what we'll do!" I exclaimed. "We'll get enough people in school to agree that telling on someone else shouldn't be a part of the honor system, so Mr. Kingman will change the rule!"

Molly stared at me, openmouthed. "Have you taken leave of your senses, Mabel? No one has changed a rule in this school since the day its doors opened! You'd have a better chance of persuading Mr. Kingman to stand on his head in the hallway."

"That might be interesting, but it wasn't what I had in mind," I retorted. "I agree with Thomas. If you don't like a law, get a new one."

"Good luck," Molly answered. "I admire your idea, but I don't think it will work."

"I've decided," I said to Sarah Jane that evening. "I'm not going to report Clarice for writing in her book. I'm going to talk to Mr. Kingman tomorrow."

Sarah Jane regarded me with horror. "Are you trying to start another Revolutionary War all by yourself? What if he's angry with you?"

"That's a chance I'll have to take. Pa says if I do what I know is right, the Lord will take care of the consequences."

But I didn't feel as brave as I sounded, and I felt even less so as I headed for Mr. Kingman's class during study period the next day. My heart was beating so hard I was sure he could hear it when I sat down beside his desk.

"What can I do for you, young lady?" he inquired pleasantly.

"Mr. Kingman, do you remember our discussion in history class yesterday about changing laws? Well, there is a part of the honor system I don't think is fair. I feel it should be changed."

Mr. Kingman lifted his eyebrows. "Oh? Suppose you tell me about it."

"Yes, sir. I'm willing to take the blame if I break the rules, but I don't think it's right to be required to tell on someone else who does."

"And may I ask why not?"

"My father says I'm only responsible for my own actions. I can't tell anyone else what to do."

"I see." Mr. Kingman seemed to be looking straight through me. "I assume you have knowledge of some wrongdoing?"

"Yes, sir."

"And you're not going to report it, is that right?"

"Yes, sir."

Mr. Kingman cleared his throat and looked very serious. "You realize that you could be subject to discipline for your action?"

I nodded miserably.

"If this wrongdoing were to endanger someone, would your, er, conscience allow you to divulge the information?"

"Oh, yes, sir," I replied eagerly. "But it doesn't. No one will be hurt but the one who ch— broke the rule."

Mr. Kingman was quiet for a long time. I thought he had forgotten about me. Finally he spoke again.

"I can't agree with you that the rule is unfair under all circumstances," he said. "But I respect your reasons in this instance.

I'm glad you've come to me." Mr. Kingman stood up. "We'll say no more about the matter."

"Thank you, Mr. Kingman. Thank you very much!"

I raced back to the room, slid into my seat, and opened a book quickly. I didn't look around, even though I could feel Molly and Sarah Jane staring at me. They would have to wait until after class to hear what had happened.

Clarice caught up with us as we walked to history.

"I told you what I'd do if you reported me, Mabel. You'll be sorry you went to Mr. Kingman." She stalked off without waiting for me to answer.

" 'The wicked flee when no man pursueth.' " Sarah Jane giggled, and then she said, "Oops, I forgot. You don't want me to quote Scripture anymore."

"That one is fine," I told her. "Just don't aim them all at me. Didn't I tell you the Lord would take care of the consequences? Worrying about when Mr. Justin is going to call her in is worse than any punishment he would give her! She's going to wish she'd just had the demerits and gotten it over with."

"I don't envy her when she has to do her translations on a test with no book to help her," Molly said. "She'll find out that cheating doesn't pay, whether the teacher knows about it or not."

I agreed, but it was hard for me to feel sorry for Clarice. She deserved the misery she brought on herself. Why was it always so hard to love one's enemies? It's so much easier to gloat over their misfortune!

5

The Most Popular Boy in School

October 16, 1889. S.J. and I have joined the Aradelphian Society. Molly has belonged to it for two years and says they have wonderful programs of speaking and music. We meet every second Friday after school and learn the fine points of elocution from Miss Baker, the sponsor. I can't wait for the first program.

MABEL, DID YOU SEE THE ANNOUNCEment on the bulletin board in the English room?" Sarah Jane caught up with me in the hallway as we started out for noon recess.

"There was nothing new there this morning."

"There is now. Molly saw Miss Baker putting a poster up, and she's gone to see what it is. Come on, let's look."

Sarah Jane grabbed my arm and dragged me toward Room 104. There were several girls standing around the board, talking excitedly. The news was printed in big, bold letters.

Aradelphian Girls

The first presentation of the year will be held in the assembly room on Friday evening, October 25, at 7:30 p.m. You may ask the young man of your choice to be your guest for this fine entertainment. Refreshments will be served.

"That's less than two weeks away!" Molly exclaimed. "We'll have to hurry!"

"Hurry for what?" Sarah Jane questioned. "It doesn't take that long to get to the assembly room." Then a horrifying thought occurred to her. "We don't have to be part of this fine entertainment, do we?"

"Of course not, silly," Molly laughed. "The society is sponsoring it. They have someone from outside for the first evening."

"Whew! That's a relief," I sighed. "I don't mind being on a program, but I want more notice than that. So why should we hurry?"

"Why, to ask a boy to be our guest," Molly replied. "If we wait, the best fellows will be taken."

We stared at her blankly. "You mean we have to walk up to some boy in school and ask him if he wants to go to the program with us?" Sarah Jane gasped.

"Certainly," Molly replied. "You wouldn't ask someone to attend and sit by himself, would you? Haven't you ever gone anywhere with a boy before?"

Sarah Jane thought this over for a moment. "Not unless you count the time I had to go to the ice-cream social with Wesley Patterson. Someone had to make sure he didn't demolish the cake he was bringing before he got there."

"I don't think I'd count that," Molly replied.

"We didn't have a large selection of boys at home to go anywhere with," I explained. "Wesley was the only one a year behind us, and Warren Carter a year ahead."

"I was thinking of asking Warren," Molly confided. "Whom are you going to invite?"

"Maybe I'll ask Thomas Charles," Sarah Jane said. "I never thought I'd be interested in a preacher's son, but he seems nice enough. Besides, Warren lives at their house, and he says Thomas is a good fellow. Warren should know—he knows everything else. What about you, Mabel?"

"I doubt if little Miss Goody has the nerve to invite anyone," a cool voice put in. "If she's never been to anything more exciting than an ice-cream social, she wouldn't know how to act." Clarice was looking right at me, and as usual I could think of nothing to say.

Sarah Jane, however, was not similarly

afflicted. "That's where you're wrong," she flared. "Mabel is going to ask the most popular boy in school to go with her. You should find out the facts before you jump to conclusions."

"You're going to ask Russ Bradley?" Clarice sneered. "You're wasting your time. He'll wait for me to invite him. Besides, what would you have to say to someone as sophisticated as Russ?"

"You needn't think you're the only knowledgeable girl in school, Clarice Owens," Sarah Jane replied. "Mabel can carry on a conversation with anyone here."

Clarice sniffed and walked away, and Sarah Jane glared at her retreating back.

"I'd feel better if I'd carried on *that* conversation," I told Sarah Jane. "Why in the world did you say I was going to invite Russ Bradley?"

"Because she needed to be brought down a peg, and that was the first thought that came to me."

"Well, I'm waiting to hear your second thought that will get me out of this," I said. "I have no intention of asking him."

"You'll have to, Mabel. Clarice will have it all over school by the time we finish eating dinner. You don't want to look bad, do you?"

"I don't see that I have a choice. How

would I look if he turned me down? Really, Sarah Jane, why didn't you just speak for yourself?"

"I wasn't the one she called 'Little Miss Goody,' " Sarah Jane replied. "No one can call my best friend names and get away with it."

"That's right," Molly agreed. "Clarice is becoming unbearable. It would serve her right if Russ did accept your invitation."

"What *is* the matter with you two?" I demanded. "You know I can't ask him! He'd laugh in my face!"

"There's always the chance that he won't," Molly said. "But you know Clarice and her friends will make life miserable for you if you back down."

"My own friends have already taken care of that," I muttered. "I'd be grateful if you didn't try to do me any more favors."

I was surprised when Russ fell into step beside me as I walked out of math class that afternoon. "That was a rough lesson today, wasn't it? Did you have any trouble with the second problem?"

"It took a long time to solve," I replied. "I hope we don't have many more like it. I have too many other things to study."

"I've noticed you and Warren Carter stay pretty close to one another in percentages.

Have you always competed with each other?"

"Since we first learned to count," I told him. "He had a year's head start on me, but I can still give him a good battle."

Russ laughed. "Do you prefer doing battle with your friends, or do you sometimes have a good time?" He didn't give me time to answer before he continued. "Speaking of good times, I heard a rumor that you were going to invite me to the Aradelphian program." His eyes twinkled, and I had the feeling he was making fun of me.

"It was strictly a rumor," I replied firmly. "I had no intention of asking you."

We walked along in silence for a moment, and then I glanced at him. "However, I wouldn't want to hurt your feelings if you were counting on it. Would you care to be my guest for the entertainment a week from Friday?"

"I would be delighted, Miss O'Dell." He gave an exaggerated bow, and then ran off across the campus to his class.

I was late and had to hurry to dress for physical culture. The others were out on the field and starting the badminton game before I got there. I was paired off with Matilda Evans, the best player in class, so I had no time to think of anything but trying to keep the shuttlecock in the air.

Molly and Sarah Jane cornered me as soon as the class was over. "We saw you talking to Russ. Did you ask him? What did you talk about?"

"We talked about how hard the math assignment was today," I replied.

They waited.

"Well," Sarah Jane prodded me. "Is that all? What about the program?"

"I should think you would have plenty to do, finding your own escorts. Haven't you already done enough for me?"

"Oh, Mabel! Sometimes you can be so infuriating." Sarah Jane stamped her foot. "Come on, Molly. It's not our fault if she goes to the program alone."

They turned to march away, and I burst out laughing.

Molly whirled around. "You *did* ask him! And he said yes! Oh, I can't wait to see Clarice's face when she finds out!"

"I can wait a long time for that," I said soberly. It suddenly occurred to me that I had provided Clarice with another reason to dislike me. "Why can't I do something to show her I'd rather be her friend? I'd be more than happy to have her go with Russ instead of me."

"Don't waste your sympathy on Clarice," Molly advised me. "She gets what she wants.

53

Just be grateful when she isn't stepping on you to get it."

"It will only be for one evening," I said to Sarah Jane later. "I think he just accepted on a dare. I'm sure he was laughing at me, and probably his friends will, too."

"I wouldn't care who laughed if I could go with a handsome boy like that." Sarah Jane sighed. "I'm going to ask Thomas. He's all right, but he's, well . . . just Thomas."

"Don't expect me to feel sorry for you," I said. "You're the one who started this whole thing."

Clarice didn't speak to me the next week, not even to make a snide remark. It made me a little nervous. "I have the feeling she's planning something to make me look bad," I told the girls. "It's not like her to let something like this just go by. I wouldn't be surprised if she persuaded Russ to change his mind and take her after all."

"She wouldn't dare," Molly declared. "She thought he'd turn you down, but it didn't work that way. Clarice has lost this round. There's nothing she can do to ruin your evening."

As it turned out, Clarice didn't need to worry about ruining anything. I almost succeeded in doing more than she could ever have thought or hoped.

"What are you wearing tonight, Mabel?" Sarah Jane asked on the morning of the program.

"My blue wool dress," I answered. "I've been saving it for a special occasion. What will you wear?"

"This wine-colored one. Ma said it was strictly for Sundays, but I think she would make an exception in this case. Besides, isn't it great to be making our own decisions? We don't have to ask anyone if we can go tonight!"

The day dragged by slowly, but it was finally time for the last class. Usually I enjoyed physical culture, but today I was in a hurry to get home.

"Mabel, would you help Matilda fold the badminton net and put things away, please?" Miss Baker requested. "I have a meeting to attend."

We hurried as fast as we could, but Sarah Jane was waiting impatiently when we finished. "Come on; don't stop to get dressed. Just put your skirt on over your bloomers and we'll go home the back way. It's quicker, and no one is going to see us."

I bundled my clothes and books together and we ran across the back field to the path through the woods. Sarah Jane scrambled over the fence and turned to wait for me. I threw my books across, but I didn't want my clothes on the ground, so I tucked them under one arm and tried to hold my skirt up with my free hand. It didn't work. When I jumped down, the back of the skirt caught on the top rail. A loud rip told me that the skirt and I had parted company.

"Oh, no!" I cried. "Help me get this off!"

"May I help?" a friendly voice said. And before I could catch my breath, Russ Bradley had freed my skirt and handed it to me. With a wave of his hand he was gone, and I stood rooted to the ground.

Sarah Jane turned me around and picked up my books. "Wrap that thing around you and hurry up," she said. "We're going to be late. We haven't too long to get ready."

"I'm not going anywhere," I said woodenly. "I'm never going anywhere again as long as I live. I was standing here in my *bloomers!*"

"Of course you're going." Sarah Jane pulled me along. "Just be thankful they weren't your underdrawers. He's seen girls in gym bloomers before."

"Not me, he hasn't. I've never been so embarrassed in my life. I couldn't show my face at that program. I'll probably not even go back to school."

My mind was made up, but I had reckoned without Sarah Jane and Lettie. They appeared at the door of our room as I lay across the bed, enjoying my misery.

"Come, Mabel," Lettie said briskly. "Get up and bathe and dress. I'll help you with your hair."

I meekly followed instructions, and when Thomas and Russ arrived, we were ready. The incident at the fence might have been a bad dream, for nothing was said about it, then or later.

"The first program of the year was a real success," I told Ma in a letter. "I asked a boy named Russ Bradley to be my guest, and we had a fine time."

To Sarah Jane's credit, I will say that she didn't tell anyone what happened, not even Molly. Now that's a true friend.

6
Thomas Gives
A Party

*OCTOBER 25, 1889. Lettie is having the La-
dies' Aid Meeting on Saturday, and S.J. and
I volunteered to serve the tea for her.*

*Next Friday is Halloween, and Thomas
announced a class party at his house. Russ
has already asked me to go with him. S.J., of
course, will be with Thomas.*

L ETTIE SURVEYED THE TABLE CRITICAL-
ly. "I guess it looks all right," she
decided. "Now be sure you ask each
lady what she wants in her tea, and hand
around the sandwiches and cakes when their
plates are empty. I'm certainly glad to have
you girls here today. I'll enjoy the meeting
much more, not worrying about serving."

"We're glad to do it," Sarah Jane assured
her. "You don't need to worry about a thing."

The ladies arrived, and we put their wraps
in the spare room. When they had all gathered in the parlor and begun their sewing,
we sat down in the dining room to wait until
Lettie called us.

"Just listen to all that chatter!" I said. "Visiting with the other ladies must be more fun than the sewing."

Over the hum of voices we heard Mrs. Owens, Clarice's mother. "I always hate it when Halloween comes around," she said. "This year is worse than ever. The mischief is starting a whole week early."

"Have you had a problem at your house, Gertrude?" someone asked.

"I should guess so! A group of boys came around last night after dark and rolled the rain barrel down the hill into the chicken coop. Then they took two big pumpkins out of the field. If Calvin hadn't gone out, there's no telling what else they'd have done." Mrs. Owens was indignant. "I can't think what parents are doing while their children are out disturbing the countryside. I'm not the sort to make trouble with my neighbors; I'd sooner suffer in silence. But it would be only right if someone informed some people of what their boys were doing."

At this, she must have looked directly at Thomas's mother, because we heard Mrs. Charles answer. "Why, Gertrude! You can't mean that you think Thomas was one of them!"

"Now, I didn't call any names," Mrs. Owens replied, "but everyone knows that ministers' sons are apt to be the ringleaders when anything like that goes on. And I do know whom I saw."

"I can't believe that Thomas was involved," Mrs. Charles said, "but I'll surely speak to him when I get home."

Sarah Jane pulled me into the kitchen. "Thomas was certainly *not* at the Owens place last night," she declared. "That's a horrid thing for that woman to say."

"It doesn't seem like something Thomas would do," I agreed, "but we couldn't know for sure if we didn't see him someplace else. I was here and you were at the school library studying."

Sarah Jane blushed.

"Uh, oh," I said. "You *weren't* at the school library studying."

"Yes, I was," she said. "And so was Thomas. But we finished early, so we sort of went for a walk. We saw some fellows running across the Owenses' field, but I don't know who they were."

"You'll have to tell Mrs. Charles, Sarah Jane. It wouldn't be fair if Thomas got into trouble for something he didn't do."

It was Sarah Jane's turn to look distressed. "I can't, Mabel! Thomas didn't have permission to be out. He was confined to his room every evening this week for getting a low grade on a math test. He said by last night he couldn't stand it any longer, so he went out his window and met me at the library. If I told Mrs. Charles that, he'd be in trouble with his father!"

Lettie called us and we had no time to discuss it again until after the ladies had left.

"If Mrs. Charles asks Thomas if he was at the Owenses' place last night, he can truthfully say no," Sarah Jane said. "But if she asks if he was out, he'll have to tell her."

"It looks to me like you'll both be in trouble. You didn't have permission to be anywhere but the library, either."

"I would have told Lettie if I'd known that Thomas was going to meet me," Sarah Jane protested. "I didn't just sneak out! But I can't tell her now, or I'd have to tell on him, too."

"You have a problem," I said. "Now it's my turn to feel a little bit glad that I'm not involved in it. That hasn't happened often in our lifetime."

On Monday Thomas confided to all of us that Mrs. Owens had come to talk to his father.

"What happened?" Sarah Jane wanted to know. "Did your father ask you about it?"

"Worse," Thomas replied. "He told Mrs. Owens I couldn't have been there, because he knew I was in my room all evening. Now I feel guilty about making him say something that wasn't true."

"Why don't you just tell him what you did?" I asked.

"That would mean trouble for Sarah Jane," Thomas said. "Besides another week of evenings in my room."

"Including Friday night?" Sarah Jane asked.

Thomas nodded. "I'm sure of it."

"Would you have to cancel the party?"

"No, I don't think he'd punish the whole class. He'd probably say that Warren could take charge of the party."

Sarah Jane sighed. "Maybe we could wait until next Saturday to tell them. That would take care of your conscience but not make you miss the party."

"If you do that, you might just end up spending the rest of your life in your room," Molly said. "Parents have a way of being sticky about things like that."

"Not to mention deceit not being high on the list of Christian virtues," Thomas said glumly. "I know I have to tell Father. I just hate to think of doing it."

"He didn't think about it very long," Warren told us the next morning. "He told his father last night. I don't know what all was said, but I know Rev. Charles believes that Thomas wasn't at the Owenses' Friday night. Thomas said his father would have to tell Mrs. Owens that he was mistaken about Thomas being in his room, though."

"That means she'll never believe that Thomas didn't roll her rain barrel into the chicken coop," Molly replied. "She believes what she wants to, even if the preacher tells her differently!"

"I suppose there'll be no party for Thomas?" Sarah Jane asked.

Warren nodded. "Just as he expected."

"I guess that's only fair punishment, but the party won't be much fun without him."

"It doesn't seem right to have a party in his barn and not have him there," Molly agreed. "But I'm sure we'll have fun. We always do."

"Is there any chance that your father will relent at the last minute?" we asked Thomas later.

"I doubt it," he replied. "If it were just between the two of us, maybe, but not with Mrs. Owens hovering in the background. She's never had much tolerance for preachers' kids, and she's finally got one where she wants him."

Halloween evening was a perfect night for a party. The harvest moon was huge and the breeze was cool. As we got ready to leave, Lettie reminded us about sweaters.

"It will be warm in the barn, but you'll get cool walking home. It was nice of Russ to offer to escort both of you."

"I feel like a tagalong," Sarah Jane grumbled, "but it was nice of him. It's better than being walked over and back by Jacob."

The big barn behind the parsonage was alive with activity when we arrived. Lanterns hung from the rafters. Pumpkin faces were lighted with candles. Corn shocks stood in the corners, and bales of hay were placed conveniently for some of the older people who had come to watch the fun. Rev. Charles was lining everyone up for a relay race.

"Put the apple on your head and run as quickly as you can across the barn and back to your row. If the apple falls, you'll have to chase it and put it back. Otherwise you can't touch it. Ready? Go!"

"Oh, my!" Molly gasped as she ran back to the line. "I chased that apple all the way over and back. It didn't stay on my head for more than three steps."

We bobbed for apples, played Skip to My Lou, and had just finished a tug-of-war when I looked toward the door and saw Mrs. Owens sailing into the barn. Warren saw her at the same time.

"Uh, oh," he said. "She doesn't look like someone who's come to enjoy the party."

She glared around the barn at the young people, who were drifting toward the big table that was loaded with food. Rev. Charles walked over to where she was.

"Good evening, Mrs. Owens. Will you join us for refreshments?"

"That's not what I came for," Mrs. Owens snapped. "Suppose you tell me where your son Thomas is *now*, Rev. Charles?"

"He wasn't allowed to attend the party," the minister replied. "He's in his room."

"Hah!" Mrs. Owens sniffed. "That's what you said last week. I've come to inform you that I saw him in my field again. You would do well to keep a closer watch on that boy, Reverend. Now what do you intend to do about him?"

"Mrs. Owens, I assure you that Thomas has not left his room. He is being punished for going out without permission. He would not do the same thing again. Would you care to come to the house to see for yourself?"

"I certainly would!" Mrs. Owens declared. She marched ahead of Rev. Charles, and Warren trailed along behind. He told us later what happened.

"Thomas," his father called, "Will you come out, please?"

There was no answer, so Rev. Charles knocked on the door and then opened it. The room was empty.

"Well?" Mrs. Owens said triumphantly.

Rev. Charles looked perplexed. "Warren, do you know where Thomas is?"

"No, sir," Warren answered. "He was here when I left, and I know he intended to stay here. He told me to come and tell him all about the party as soon as it was over."

Just then the back door opened, and Thomas came up the stairs. His face and hands were black with soot.

"Thomas! What happened? Where have you been?"

"I'm sorry I left, Father," Thomas replied, "but I had to. I was looking out the window when I saw the haystack in the Owenses' field catch fire. I didn't have time to come and get you. I ran over and helped Mr. Owens put it out before it spread to his barn."

Rev. Charles put his arms around Thomas and hugged him. Mrs. Owens muttered something about needing to get home and hurried out the door.

"Come on, boys," the minister said. "There's lots of food out there, and we'd better hurry if we're going to get our share."

"I hope that woman tells you she's sorry

for accusing you," Sarah Jane said to Thomas on the way home.

"It's all right if she doesn't," Thomas replied. "At least Mr. Owens caught the boys responsible. I'm just glad to have my name cleared."

"Not to mention the fact that you got in on the good food," Russ added. "It was a great party, Thomas. But the next time you give one, try to attend the whole thing!"

7

A Thump
On the Head

NOVEMBER 17, 1889. Winter is here at last. We've had several big snowfalls, and it looks like more today.

Midterm exams start this week. As usual, I'm nervous about them, but I'm trying to do as Ma advised—study as hard as I can and trust the Lord to bring things to mind.

I DON'T THINK I FEEL VERY WELL THIS morning," I said.

"I'm not surprised," Sarah Jane replied. "You tossed and moaned all night long. Did you eat something that didn't agree with you?"

"No, I dreamed something that didn't agree with me. I failed all my exams."

"There's no way you could fail an exam, Mabel. You don't know how."

"It didn't seem too hard in my dream. I just didn't write anything."

"Dreams do not happen when you're awake," Sarah Jane assured me. "By Wednesday you'll have forgotten it and be writing more than anyone in the class."

I knew it was foolish to be bothered by a dream, but it kept coming back to me all day. It didn't help when Warren joined us at noon.

"I suppose you're all ready for the big week," he said cheerfully. "You've kept up with me pretty well on the daily lessons. Do you think you can do as well on the exams?"

"Oh, Warren, go plague someone else, will you please?" I said crossly. "You know there isn't one-tenth of a percentage point between us. Why wouldn't I do well?"

"I can always hope, can't I? You could be hit in the head and lose your memory, or . . ."

"If you don't get out of here, I'm likely to hit *you* in the head," I told him. "Don't waste your time wishing misfortune on me. If you can't stand the thought of a girl being as smart as you are, that's your problem."

The examination schedule was posted on the bulletin board. I had two days to go over my notes and listen to the review in classes. There was no reason why I should have any difficulty, but I felt uneasy.

"That schedule isn't going to disappear because you're glaring at it." Russ stood beside me, and I hadn't even heard him approach. "You look as though you could use some fresh air. How about going tobogganing with us this evening?"

"Thanks, Russ." I shook my head. "I'd better not. I should stay in and study."

"Still competing with Warren, huh? Well, if you change your mind, be ready when we come to pick up Sarah Jane."

He walked away, and I turned to start home. Sarah Jane was staying to complete a science project, and I'd have a couple of hours before supper to work. *What makes him think keeping ahead of Warren is all I care about?* I thought irritably. I was concerned about my own record, after all.

I started reviewing my Latin. That needed the least time, I thought, and getting the easy ones out of the way first would leave time for history and math. I was so immersed in my book that the sound of Lettie's voice startled me.

"Mabel, it's too dark in here to see. Why haven't you lighted the lamp?"

"I didn't even notice," I replied. "Is it getting that late? Where's Sarah Jane?"

"She's coming up the road. Suppose you put that aside now; supper's almost ready."

"I guess I will, Lettie. My back is getting stiff from sitting still so long." I got up and stretched the kinks out, and then went downstairs to meet Sarah Jane. She came in covered with snow.

"It's beautiful out there!" she exclaimed.

"It's going to be great for sledding tonight."

I looked out the door. "When did that start?"

"What do you mean, when did it start? Where've you been all afternoon?"

"Studying," I replied. "I didn't have time to look out the window." I took her books while she removed her coat and boots. "You're going tobogganing tonight?"

"Of course! Who could stay in on a night like this just to study?"

"I could," I told her. "You would, too, if you'd had the dream I had."

"Are you still worried about that?" Sarah Jane looked at me in disbelief. "You know dreams have nothing to do with what really happens. Besides, you need some time to let your brain rest. Come on. Even Warren is going tonight."

"Sarah's right, Mabel. You need to get out for a while," Lettie agreed. "Come and eat supper, and then put on your warm things and go with the other young people. A couple of hours will refresh your mind so you can think better when you come back."

By the time the others had arrived, I was convinced that I shouldn't miss the party.

"Aren't you glad you came?" Russ asked during one of our plodding trips back up the hill. I nodded happily. It really was a beauti-

71

ful night to be out. At the top of the ridge, four of us climbed on the toboggan for another ride to the bottom.

Later, I remembered that we were going down a different slide, and someone called, "Look out!" The next thing I knew, I was waking up in Dr. Matson's office. Molly, Sarah Jane, Russ, and Warren stood around me with anxious faces.

"Oh, you frightened us, Mabel!" Molly said. "You looked so pale, I thought you were dead!"

"I knew she wasn't dead. She'd never miss her exams," Sarah Jane said.

"I'm sorry I said anything about hitting your head," Warren put in. "Can you still think?"

"And I shouldn't have made that remark about your competing with Warren, either," Russ added. "I just wanted you to come with us."

"I don't suppose anyone wants to tell me what happened, do you?" I asked. "How did I get here?"

"Your toboggan hit a rock, and all of you were thrown off," Dr. Matson said. "Unfortunately, you landed on your head against a tree. If it hadn't been for your heavy hat and the scarf tied over it, you'd probably have cracked your skull open. The boys pulled you over here on the sled. You'd better not try walking for a while."

"How long a while?" I asked anxiously. "I have to go to school tomorrow."

Dr. Matson shook his head. "No school for you this week, young lady. At least five days in bed. Lettie will see that you're taken care of."

"But I have to take my exams!" I wailed.

"They'll be there when you get back," Dr. Matson assured me. "Your teachers will let you make them up. I don't want you looking at any books this week. Take this medicine, and we'll get you home to bed."

My head ached so badly that I knew it was no use to protest. Perhaps if I lay perfectly still, I would be well sooner than the doctor expected.

I slept most of the next day. Lettie came in to check on me and reported that the world was going around very nicely without me. Sarah Jane offered to read my history notes to me in the afternoon, and Molly came by to say that our classmates sent their sympathy.

On Wednesday morning I made a tentative effort to get up alone. I could see at once that I would not be going anywhere.

"Why did the Lord let something happen to me right now?" I asked Lettie when she came in. "He knows this is exam week."

"I'm not sure I can answer that, child," Lettie replied. "Maybe he wants you to know that there are things in life just as important as being at the head of your class."

"But surely God wants us to do the very best we can!"

"You've done that, haven't you?"

"Yes," I answered. "I've tried to. I can't see how that could be wrong."

"Maybe you've been trying for the wrong reasons," Lettie suggested.

She left me to think that over. What wrong reason was there for wanting to be a good student? Or even the *best* student?

Sarah Jane came home in the afternoon with a report on the first two tests. "You won't have any trouble with English or biology, Mabel. They both covered exactly what we had in class. Warren is just going to have to wait an extra week until you take your exams before he finds out who's at the top. Everyone knows it will be one or the other of you."

Suddenly I knew what Lettie meant. Just learning all I could wasn't enough for me. I had to be better than someone else. My pride would be hurt if Warren earned a few points more than I did, even if I had done my best.

"A thump on the head is a pretty hard way to learn that," Sarah Jane said when I shared the insight with her. "Does that mean you won't be competing with Warren any longer?"

"It doesn't mean that I won't try to be first if I can," I told her. "I just won't think the sky has fallen on me if he does better. At least I hope that's how I'll feel. I really don't like to be second."

On Monday I returned to school and was told that I might make up my exams, one each day, after my classes.

"Are you sure you didn't arrange that accident so you could know what was on the tests before you took them?" Clarice asked. "I was just kidding," she added with a laugh. "You probably didn't need that extra week to study."

"I'd almost forgotten what a pain she is," I sputtered to Molly. "If I were going to arrange an accident, I'd have it happen to her."

"So that's what it means to love your neighbor as yourself," Molly laughed. "You'd share whatever you have with her—even a broken head!"

"No, that's not love," I admitted. "That's spite. I'm going to have to pray that the Lord will help me be forgiving toward her, or I'll end up acting just like she does. I wish I knew why she dislikes me so."

"Why not ask her?" Molly suggested. "My

theory is that she wants to be the most popular girl in school. You're in her way."

The similarity between Clarice and me was plainer than I wanted to look at just then. I pushed the thought away and concentrated on studying. When the grades were posted, Warren and I shared first place in everything but math. Again he was ahead by two points.

"I really think I've learned something this term," I confided to Sarah Jane. "Trying to keep ahead of someone else takes all the fun out of what you're doing."

"I've known that for a long time," Sarah Jane told me. "Ever since first grade I've never been able to get ahead of you, so I just settle for having fun! We mediocre people have so much less trouble going through life, Mabel. You really ought to try it."

I made a face at her and settled down to read a new book. The second term had begun on Monday, and I determined to put my newfound knowledge to work. I would begin having fun.

8
A Honey
Of an Idea

NOVEMBER 25, 1889. Thanksgiving is over and there are just a few weeks until Christmas. We're trying to think of something nice to give Lettie and Jacob. S.J. thinks doing something would be good, but we haven't decided what it could be.

"MABEL, HAVE YOU NOTICED THAT Lettie looks awfully tired lately?" Sarah Jane looked up from her book to ask the question.

"I guess I have," I replied, "but I didn't know whether she was tired or worried about something. Maybe we're more of a burden on her than we think."

"How could nice, sensible young ladies like us be a burden to anyone?" Sarah Jane said with a laugh. "I'll admit she has more work than she'd have if we weren't here, but Lettie seems to thrive on work. If she doesn't have any to do, she makes it up."

Just then Lettie called up the stairs. "Girls, would you like some hot chocolate?"

"Let's see if we can find out what's bothering her," I said as we ran downstairs to join Lettie and Jacob in the kitchen.

"I'm glad we're not delegated to the dining room to eat any longer," Sarah Jane said as we sipped the hot drink.

"We didn't know whether you'd want to be bothered with two old codgers like us," Jacob said. "I know what a nice fellow I am, but I've been Lettie's brother all these years, and I'm still not sure about her." His eyes twinkled, and he grinned happily at Lettie.

"Oh, go on with you," she replied. "We just wanted you girls to know that this was your home, and you were free to do as you wanted. I had thought you might prefer to eat by yourselves."

I shook my head. "We like it much better out here with you. The dining room makes us feel like company. Lettie, are we too much work for you?"

Lettie looked surprised. "Work? I should say not. I don't know what we'd have done, the two of us rattling around this big place all winter. Jacob prefers his rooms over the carriage house, and I'd have been all alone in the house without you two girls."

"We just thought you looked sort of tired," Sarah Jane explained. "We can help out more, if you are."

"No," Lettie replied. "I'm not tired. I've been a mite concerned about our sister Emma, but I haven't seen my way clear to go visit her lately."

"She only lives about sixty miles away, doesn't she?" Sarah Jane asked. "You could get there on the train in a couple of hours."

"I know, but it would be more than a one-day trip," Lettie said. "I couldn't be away more than a day."

"I don't know why not," Jacob put in. "I daresay the three of us could keep the house standing for a few days."

"Of course, we could!" I said. "You could go on the Friday afternoon train and come back Sunday evening. We'd manage just fine!"

"Well, I don't know," Lettie began doubtfully. "I suppose I might leave food that you could shove in the oven or heat up easily—"

"That's a great idea, Lettie!" Sarah Jane exclaimed. "We know how to take care of meals and dishes, and Jacob would be here in case we needed anything. You go ahead and visit your sister. What could go wrong?"

It was soon settled that Lettie would leave the next Friday.

"You should never have said, 'What could go wrong?' " I told Sarah Jane as we went back upstairs. "That does nothing but tempt fate."

"Oh, Mabel," she scoffed, "don't be silly. You know we don't believe in fate. The Lord directs our paths, and he's certainly watched over us in the past. Besides, we're becoming quite mature, and I don't have any qualms at all about being in charge for the weekend."

Lettie was ready to leave when we arrived home from school on Friday. After lengthy directions as to what food there was to eat and how to prepare it, she followed Jacob to the buggy.

"Will it be all right if Molly spends the night with us tonight?" Sarah Jane asked. "We'll stay in and play games."

"I think that would be nice," Lettie answered. "You might make some taffy and popcorn. Have a nice time, and I'll see you Sunday evening."

We waved as they left for the station, and then went to put our books away.

"Let's go over and get Molly right away," Sarah Jane suggested. "We'll have a nice long evening to have fun."

Mrs. Matson was a little uneasy. "Are you sure you girls will be all right with Lettie gone? You will be sensible, won't you?"

"Oh, Mama!" Molly protested. "We aren't babies! Jacob is there if we need anything, and Lettie said it would be fine."

Mrs. Matson didn't look too convinced, but

she said no more. We left in high spirits, excited over the evening ahead.

Lettie had put potatoes and a meat loaf in the oven to bake. We worked together to fix a vegetable, slice bread, and cut the pie for supper. Sarah Jane undertook the job of brewing coffee for Jacob.

"Don't know when I've had a better meal," he pronounced when he had finished, "or better company to eat it with. And that coffee was strong enough to go out and find a job on its own. You ladies did right well." He pushed back his chair. "I'll build up the fire for you, and then I'll be going back out to my room. I can come in and close up and bank the stove before I go to bed, if you like."

"Oh, no," we assured him. "We can take care of everything. And we'll have your breakfast ready at the usual time."

Jacob brought in more wood, put on his hat and coat, and headed for the carriage house. We quickly cleared up the kitchen, and then got out a game of dominoes and set it up on the table. It wasn't until the clock struck eight that Sarah Jane remembered the taffy.

"Let's stop and make it now," she suggested. "Molly, you pop some corn, and we'll get the stuff for the candy."

I rummaged in the kitchen cupboard for pans, and Sarah Jane went to the pantry in search of butter and brown sugar for the taffy.

"There isn't enough brown sugar here," she called. "What'll we do?"

"We can put molasses with it," I replied. "I think Lettie has some in the storage room out back. I'll go get it." I found the molasses and something else. "Look here," I said.

The girls came to see. "Oh, it's the honey that has sugared," Sarah Jane said. "I heard Lettie say just the other day she didn't have much honey left that she could use. She wished she had that melted down so she could cook with it."

"Why don't we do it for her and surprise her when she gets home?" I suggested. "It's only five gallons, and we can lift it with all three of us helping. We'll just put it on the back of the stove and it can melt slowly."

Carefully we lifted the big metal container of honey and set it on the stove. Then we popped the corn and boiled the molasses, brown sugar, and butter for the candy. By the time we were finished with our treat, it was time to go to bed.

"We'll check the doors and close the damper on the stove, and everything will be ready for the night," Sarah Jane said. "I'll carry the lamp and you can each bring a warming brick for the beds."

Molly felt the side of the honey can. "It's just barely warm," she said. "But do you think we should pry the top up a little before we leave it? Does honey expand or contract when it's heated?"

None of us knew, so just to be safe I loosened the cap on the spout so that steam could escape. "I don't care to hear that pop off in the night," I said. "It will be all right now."

We brought a cot into our room and made up a bed for Molly. It seemed like only minutes after we'd fallen asleep that I felt someone poking me.

"Mabel," Sarah Jane whispered. "Are you awake?"

"Not by choice," I replied. "Why are *you* awake? Are you sick?"

"No, but I think I smell something. Do you smell anything?"

"You can always smell *something*," I replied. "What kind of anything are you talking about?"

By this time Molly was awake. "What's the matter?" she said. "Is someone sick?"

"Not yet, but I think I'm about to be," Sarah Jane said. "I smell something."

Molly and I both sat up and sniffed the air.

"Something is baking," Molly decided.

"The *honey*!" I cried, and all three of us

leapt from the beds and headed for the door.

"The lamp!" Sarah Jane yelled. "We can't go down without a light." We all dashed for the lamp on the dresser and collided in the middle of the room.

"We'll have to calm down," Molly said sensibly. "Light the lamp and we'll go to the kitchen together."

After several tries the lamp was lighted, and we ran to the stairs. The sweet odor of honey became stronger as we descended.

"We didn't put on our wrappers or house shoes." Sarah Jane's teeth chattered. "We'll freeze down here."

"We can't go back now," I said. "The kitchen will be warm."

And indeed it was. Warm and sweet and sticky. We huddled in the doorway and stared at the sight before us. Honey bubbled gently and silently out of the spout, over the sides of the tin, down the stove, and across the kitchen floor.

"What are we going to do?" Sarah Jane moaned.

"We have got to get that honey off the stove!" Molly declared emphatically, and she waded resolutely into the sticky mess.

"It's *hot*!" I warned her. "We can't lift it down. It would slop all over the floor!"

They both looked at me.

"Well, worse than it is now."

"Shall we pour water in the stove and put the fire out?" Molly said.

"That wouldn't work," Sarah Jane replied. "It takes hours for the stove top to cool. We'll just have to call Jacob to take it off. You go, Mabel."

"I knew that 'we' didn't mean all of us," I muttered. "I can't go back upstairs with sticky feet, and I'm not going out in the snow in bare ones."

"We can't just stand here and watch that honey pour out of the spout," Sarah Jane said in despair. "Here—put on Lettie's old garden boots."

There seemed to be no way around it, so I stuck my honey-covered feet into the boots and ran for the carriage house.

Jacob dressed quickly, and within seconds he was standing at the back door.

"Oh, my," he said. "Oh my, oh my. I should have stayed in bed."

Briskly he donned a pair of heavy gloves, carried the honey can outside, and placed it in the snow. Then he returned to survey the kitchen.

"If there's anywhere that stuff hasn't gone, I fail to see it," he said. "I suppose you had a very good reason for putting honey on a hot stove, but I don't see that, either. We might as well get busy and clean it up." He looked at us huddled around the stove. "Can't say as you're dressed for the job, but there's no backing out of it now."

"Where do we start?" Sarah Jane wailed. "I don't even know what to do!"

"Maybe we could put snow on the floor and shovel the honey out with it," Molly suggested.

"Not a bad idea," Jacob nodded. "You girls get soap melted and water hot for scrubbing, and I'll shovel."

As the clock struck two, we wearily washed our feet and headed back upstairs. Jacob had assured us that he would say nothing to Lettie, and that she would be happy to have her honey melted down.

"Of course, she thought she had more than one gallon in that can," he chuckled. "She may wonder a bit about that."

Lettie returned Sunday, rested and reassured. "You got along just fine, did you?" she said as we carried her things into the house. "It's good to be back." She sniffed appreciatively. "Smells good in here. Did you bake something while I was gone?"

"No," I said. "We ate just what you left us. We're glad to have you back, too."

Lettie headed for the kitchen. "How about nice hot biscuits and honey for supper?"

Jacob leaned against the stair rail and bit his lip to keep from laughing. Sarah Jane clapped her hand over her mouth. From the kitchen we heard Lettie's voice as she talked to herself.

"Now how in the world did this honey get behind my stove?"

9
An Error
In Judgment

January 7, 1890. We are back after a wonderful Christmas at home. S.J.'s aunt and uncle are delayed back East, so we are still under Lettie's care. It was easier to leave home this time—we really looked forward to coming back to school.

WHERE DID I LEAVE MY MITTENS?"
"Downstairs in the hallway, Sarah." Lettie's voice came from outside our open door. "I put them on the hall tree."

"Thank you, Lettie. Come on, Mabel. We're going to be late."

We rushed out the door, bundled against the cold.

"From the looks of things so far, it's going to be a long winter," I said, shivering. "We won't be walking to school through the woods until spring unless we take a shovel with us."

We hurried along in silence for a while. "Why do you suppose Lettie never calls you

Sarah Jane," I wondered. "She hasn't since the day we came."

"I suppose she thinks it's a waste of words," Sarah Jane replied. "I'm surprised she doesn't call me Jane; that has only one syllable. I've noticed that Lettie doesn't waste much of anything."

When we opened the big front door of the school, we found the students milling about in the corridor instead of going into the classrooms.

"I thought we were late," Sarah Jane said. "What's everyone doing out here?"

Molly hurried over to us. "Something is wrong with the heating system," she reported. "The building is so cold that Mr. Kingman says it wouldn't be practical to stay. We have a whole day free!"

"Oh, my goodness!" I exclaimed. "What do we do with unexpected riches like that? Besides study, that is."

"I'm sure you'll think of something useful," Clarice put in. "Don't you have some unfinished chores somewhere?"

I had already decided that her remarks weren't worth answering, so I started to walk away. But Clarice wasn't finished. "Some of us are going down to have our ears pierced. But I don't suppose you'd be brave enough for that kind of wickedness, would you?" She looked at all three of us this time. Then, with a haughty smile, she walked off with her friends.

"Do you think she means it?" Sarah Jane asked. "Where would she go?"

"The only place I know is the dry goods store," said Molly. "There's a lady there who will pierce your ears if you buy some little gold earrings. A lot of the older girls have had it done, but I don't know anyone in school who has."

We slowly followed the others out the door. "I think we should do it, too," Sarah Jane declared. "Do you want to?"

"I will if you will," Molly answered. They both looked at me.

"I guess sixteen isn't too young," I said slowly. "We are old enough to be on our own. Maybe we should take our books home and tell Lettie why school is out. Then we could go."

I wasn't sure about the wisdom of what we were planning, and I thought perhaps they'd change their minds if we put it off awhile.

"All right," Molly said. "Come right back to my house as soon as you see Lettie. We'll show Clarice that she isn't the only brave one around."

We promised and then turned toward home. "I can't figure out why Clarice aims all her little barbs at me," I said. "Why doesn't she pick on you once in a while?"

"Because she knows that I would kick her in the shins," Sarah Jane answered calmly.

"Don't think it hasn't crossed my mind," I replied. "I keep thinking I should find a soft answer. But instead I end up with no answer at all, getting more put out with her by the minute. If it weren't for her superior attitude, I might not have the nerve to get my ears pierced. That's one thing I never thought to ask Ma if I could do."

"We can make our own decisions now, Mabel. We don't have to ask permission every time we leave the house."

One part of me agreed and the other part remembered the day I'd made my own decision to wear my good dress to school. Somehow pierced ears seemed to be even more permanent than the ink stain on my dress had been.

"Lettie, we're back," Sarah Jane called when we entered the house. There was no answer, and the house seemed strangely silent.

"Lettie, where are you?" We pushed open the door from the dining room and went down the few stairs to the kitchen. It was empty.

It had occurred to me that it might be well

to ask Lettie's advice before we left.

"She's probably still upstairs," I said. "Let's go put our books away." But Lettie was nowhere to be seen.

"She's gone out to the barn to see Jacob," Sarah Jane decided. "Come on, we'll tell her we're going to Molly's."

Jacob was mending harnesses when we entered the warm barn. He looked up in surprise. "I declare! This is the shortest day I can remember. Are you home from school already?"

"Yes," I laughed, "but not because the day is over. There was no heat at school. And there's no Lettie in the house. Do you know where she is?"

"Lettie? I expect she's gone on an errand. Did you need something?"

"Just tell her where we're going. We'll be at Molly's."

"I wouldn't be surprised if I could remember that. I'll give her the message," he said.

"Did you tell your mother where we're going?" I asked Molly as we started toward town.

"Yes, but I didn't tell her what we were planning to do. I figured this was something your folks couldn't make you take back if they didn't like it. As Shakespeare says, 'What's done is done.'"

"I don't think I'd have the nerve to do it without asking if my mother were here," Sarah Jane said. "I'm not very skilled at this independence business yet."

It took just a few minutes to have our ears pierced and the new earrings put in place. We were pleased with the results, and I pushed back the thought that I should have considered longer before following the lead of the others.

"We have time to look around a little before we go home," Molly said. "Did you say you'd be back for dinner this noon? Mama would like you to come and eat with us."

We spent the rest of the morning wandering in and out of the stores, imagining what it would be like to buy everything we fancied. When it was time to start for home, Molly began to slow down.

"I'm glad you're coming with me," she said. "Mama will see that I'm not the only one foolish enough to get my ears pierced."

"Foolish?" Sarah Jane stopped and looked at her. "You didn't mention that when we first talked about doing it. I hope your folks aren't going to be mad at you."

"No, not mad. Upset, maybe. Or worse yet, disappointed."

Sarah Jane and I exchanged glances. We knew about that kind of response to our escapades. Sometimes we thought mad would be easier to take.

Mrs. Matson shook her head when she saw us. "If you were determined to do that, Molly, you should have let your father pierce your ears for you. You know how doctors feel about sterile instruments. I hope none of you develops an infection."

We hadn't thought of that possibility, and now I was heartily sorry I had been so hasty.

"Papa will take care of them for you after dinner," Mrs. Matson continued. "Antiseptic after it's done will be better than no precaution at all."

"There's a lot about young girls that I don't understand," Dr. Matson muttered as he worked. "What in the world are rings in your ears good for anyway?"

"Just to look pretty, Papa," Molly told him. "They don't have to be good for something."

"I'm afraid Pa isn't going to believe that looking pretty is reason enough," I said to Sarah Jane as we walked home that afternoon. "I don't think either he or Ma is going to be happy about this."

Sarah Jane nodded. "I was thinking the same thing. But if we don't wear the earrings at home, maybe they won't notice the holes."

"You mean wear them here and take them off at home?" I thought about that for a moment. "That would be hypocrisy. We'll just have to decide what's best for us, and then go ahead and do it. I wouldn't feel right doing something Ma disapproved of behind her back."

"I know," Sarah Jane sighed. "Neither would I. The stuff you learn when you're little sure stays with you, doesn't it?"

"What are we going to tell them when they want to know why we had this done?" I wondered.

"I suppose we'll just say that we wanted to do what everyone else was doing. That's not much of a reason, but no one really wants to be different." Sarah Jane was quiet for a moment. "We can't even blame it on Clarice. We didn't have to prove anything to her."

Lettie was home when we arrived. "I see you had a busy holiday," she remarked after a glance at our earrings.

"Do you think they're pretty, Lettie?" I asked. "Molly's folks thought it was a foolish thing to do, but they didn't scold."

"I'd say you were old enough to make your own mistakes," Lettie replied.

"I don't think Ma is going to be that calm about it," Sarah Jane said. "She'll be more likely to call it a gross error in judgment."

I nodded. "And since there's nothing they can do now, they'll just say tsk, tsk every time they think about it."

"Well, this is one mistake we can make only once, if there's any satisfaction in that," Sarah Jane said.

"You'll find others," Lettie predicted dryly. "The year isn't half over yet."

10

Coals of
Fire

FEBRUARY 10, 1890. I am utterly devastated. My project that is due in English class tomorrow morning has disappeared. I can't even remember where I saw it last. It took three weeks to complete, so there's no way to do it over in time.

THINK, MABEL! YOU HAVE TO KNOW what you did with a notebook that's three inches thick!" Sarah Jane looked annoyed and anguished at the same time.

"I'm thinking, I'm thinking," I told her. "I have absolutely no idea what could have happened to it. I usually leave the work that's finished in my study desk, but I've taken everything out of there at least a dozen times."

"It certainly isn't in this house," Sarah Jane sighed. "We've turned everything upside down. Lettie has even searched her kitchen. Don't you even remember whether you took it to school or not?"

I shook my head. "No, but I must have. Maybe it fell out of my desk and the janitor swept it up."

Sarah Jane didn't believe that was possible, but she had no other ideas to offer. "You've been forgetful in the past," she grumbled, "but this is ridiculous. You've had that thing under your nose for a month and suddenly, on the day it's due, it disappears."

"You're not doing a whole lot to make me feel better," I snapped. "I don't need a sermon on top of worrying about what to do."

"I know, Mabel. I'm sorry. Maybe you could ask Miss Baker for an extension of time and do it over."

"This is worse than having to tell Pa I lost the buggy when I was seven years old," I moaned. "But I guess I don't have a choice."

Monday morning's English class came too soon for me, and Miss Baker's announcement did nothing to cheer me up.

"Your semester project is due today. Every day that it is late will reduce your grade one full point. An A notebook turned in tomorrow will receive a B. There will be no exceptions."

"In other words, unless I find it by Wednesday, there's no point in even turning it in," I said to Molly and Sarah Jane after class.

"You could get a D on Thursday," Molly pointed out. "That's one grade point."

"I've never had a D in my entire life," I said. "It might as well be an F."

"I still think you should explain to her," Sarah Jane said. "You could at least tell her you had done it."

After physical culture class, Miss Baker called to me. "I didn't find your English notebook, Mabel. You did hand it in, didn't you?"

"I can't find it," I said miserably. "I've looked everywhere I can think of, here and at home. I'll keep looking and turn it in as soon as I can."

Miss Baker nodded sympathetically. "I'm sure you've finished it, and I wish I could give you more time. It wouldn't be fair to the others, though. If you find it by this evening, bring it to my home. I'll accept it for today's grade."

Sarah Jane went with me to go through my study desk again, even though I knew it wasn't there. "I wish I dared to go through every desk in this room," she declared. "It might have gotten into one of them by mistake."

"Oh, we couldn't do that," I exclaimed. "Besides, someone would have found it by now. I'd know if there were something that big in my desk that didn't belong to me."

"That notebook didn't grow legs and walk away," Lettie declared that evening. "And it isn't going to do you any good to just push your food around your plate and starve yourself over it. When you've done all you can, leave it with the Lord and go on about your business."

That seemed like reasonable advice, and I tried to eat my supper and study as usual. I was worried, though, and it was hard to keep from thinking about it.

On Wednesday morning during study hall, Clarice poked me in the back. "Is this what you've been looking for?" she asked, holding out my English notebook.

"Where did you get that?" I shouted, and everyone looked at me in amazement. Mrs. Gates walked back to my desk.

"What on earth is the matter?" she asked.

"Clarice had my notebook in her desk, and it was due on Monday," I sputtered. I turned to Clarice. "Did you know it was there all this time?"

She shrugged. "What are you getting so upset about? You'll at least get a C. What if I hadn't found it until Friday?"

"How in the world did it get in her desk in the first place?" Sarah Jane said at lunchtime.

"I think she took it out of mine just for pure spite," I said. "She wanted to see me get a poor grade."

"You may be right," Molly agreed. "She looked too happy for it to be a mistake. What are you going to do about it?"

"Do? What can I do? There's nothing that will get my grade back."

"I certainly wouldn't let her get away with it," Molly replied. "I'd find some way to pay her back."

"We were brought up believing you should pray for those that despitefully use you," Sarah Jane said. "I'll admit it isn't always the easiest way to take care of things, but it works."

"The only thing I could pray for her right now is that the Lord would heap coals of fire on her head," I declared. "I don't feel a great deal of love in my heart for Clarice."

I was still thinking about it that evening as we did our homework. "What is it that the Bible says about coals of fire?" I said. "I think I'll look it up."

I found the reference in the concordance and turned to chapter twelve of Romans. My eye fell on verse nineteen. "Listen to this," I said to Sarah Jane. "It says here, 'Dearly beloved, avenge not yourselves, but rather give place unto wrath: for it is written,

Vengeance is mine; I will repay, saith the Lord.' "

"It doesn't say he won't send you with the payment," Sarah Jane said. "What about the coals of fire?"

" 'Therefore if thine enemy hunger; feed him; if he thirst, give him drink: for in doing so thou shalt heap coals of fire on his head,' " I read. "That wasn't exactly what I had in mind. It sounds as though you can't just dump the coals on someone; you have to do something good for him. Is that how it sounds to you?"

"I guess so," she admitted. "If you do something good for people who don't deserve it, they'll be sorry for the way they acted."

"That's what is *supposed* to happen," I said. "I'm just not sure it will work that way with Clarice."

"You aren't responsible for Clarice," Lettie told me when I mentioned it to her. "You are only responsible for doing what you know is right. The Lord will take care of the rest."

"That's what Pa always said. But I don't know what to do for her."

"I think I'd start out by forgiving her," Lettie suggested. "If I'm not mistaken, that's the last thing she'd expect."

"That's easier to say than to do," I confided to Sarah Jane. "I don't feel like forgiving her.

Sometimes I think the Bible is too hard on us."

By the end of the week I was so angry about what Clarice had done that I was even snapping at my friends.

"Clarice is going around as happy as a lark, and you're getting grumpier by the day," Molly said. "It seems to me you've heaped the coals of fire on your own head."

I glared at Molly and didn't reply, but I knew she was right. Until I forgave Clarice, I was going to feel worse than she did. The following week the notebooks were returned, and my grade was a C. I had made up my mind that I would forgive Clarice whether I wanted to or not, just because I knew I should. When class was over I turned to face her.

"Clarice, I want you to know that I forgive you for taking my notebook," I said.

She looked surprised. "You don't need to bother. I didn't take it," she replied.

"Then who did? Someone had to remove it from my desk."

"Don't ask me," she shrugged. "It was just as I told you. I found it in my desk."

By this time, Molly and Sarah Jane had stopped to listen. "But you didn't just find it there on Wednesday, did you?" Molly said accusingly.

"Well, no," Clarice admitted reluctantly. "I found it Monday morning. But I didn't think it would hurt Mabel to get a C for once. She can find out how ordinary people feel."

"I can't believe you, Clarice Owens!" I exclaimed. "You deliberately kept my notebook so I'd get a lower grade! That was just as bad as taking it!"

"I suppose it was," she replied airily. "But since you've already forgiven me, it doesn't matter, does it? Unless you're going to take it back?"

I opened my mouth to tell her that she didn't deserve to be forgiven, when I suddenly remembered all the times my family and friends had forgiven me, even when I hadn't asked for it.

"No, I won't take it back. I truly do forgive you, Clarice. I don't know why you dislike me so much, but I won't hold it against you."

To my surprise, tears came to her eyes. Without a word she turned and left the room.

"What do you know?" Molly breathed. "She actually has a conscience!"

"I feel sorry for her," I said. "I didn't before, but I do now. Anyone who acts like that must feel really awful inside."

A few days later Miss Baker called me to her desk. "I found out what happened to your notebook, Mabel. The janitor found it on the floor and put it where he thought it belonged. This morning Clarice told me what she had done. Under the circumstances it wouldn't be fair to penalize you, so I'll raise your grade. I'm sorry this happened. I know how worried you were."

"I'm glad about the grade," I said to Sarah Jane and Molly, "but I'd feel better if Clarice could be a friend instead of an enemy."

"Don't hold your breath," Molly said. "Even the girls she runs around with never know whether she's going to be friendly or not. It all depends on how she happens to feel when she gets up in the morning."

I didn't plan to hold my breath, but I was determined to do what I could to win Clarice over. If she couldn't like me, there had to be some way to make her at least tolerate me.

11

An Unwelcome Guest

FEBRUARY 11, 1890. We have had a most horrendous week. S.J. and I have had our patiences tried to the absolute limit. We have a guest in the house, and even Jacob is beginning to look haunted.

"DO YOU WANT TO KNOW WHAT'S steaming up the path?" It was time to leave for school, and Sarah Jane was looking out the window as she waited for me to be ready.

"Not really," I replied, "but I'm sure you're going to tell me anyway."

"Mrs. Owens."

I rushed to the window. "What could she want at this hour of the morning?"

"Nothing good," Sarah Jane predicted, "although that has nothing to do with the time of day. She just radiates bad news."

We heard the door knocker and Lettie admitting the visitor, but from our room it was impossible to hear the conversation going on below.

"I'm going to hang over the banister," Sarah Jane declared.

"You can't do that!" I protested. "That's eavesdropping! Besides, Lettie will probably tell us about it soon enough."

I was right. As soon as the door closed on Mrs. Owens's departing back, Lettie called to us.

"Girls, I have something to discuss with you before you leave for school."

"We'll be right down, Lettie," I replied. I turned to Sarah Jane. "Think fast. What have we done to Clarice lately that would bring her mother here to complain?"

"The only thing I ever do is ignore her," Sarah Jane said. "She shouldn't complain about that—she doesn't know how lucky she is."

We descended the stairs and found Lettie standing in the hallway, her face grim.

"Mrs. Owens was just here," she stated. "Her mother is very ill, and Gertrude and Mr. Owens must go to be with her. She wants Clarice to stay here while she is gone."

Sarah Jane gasped. "In this house? With us?"

Lettie nodded. "She said there was no other place to leave her. The minister's house has all boys, and every other place I suggested had something wrong with it.

Gertrude insisted that Mrs. Clark would feel it was her duty to care for Clarice, so I had no choice."

"She's probably right about Aunt Rhoda," Sarah Jane agreed. "She's always been partial to strays. Where is Clarice going to sleep?"

"I'll fix up the spare room," Lettie sighed. "We'll have to do our best to make her feel welcome. Her father will bring her things over today, and she'll come home with you after school."

"Offhand, I can't think of anything that could ruin my day faster than news like that," I said as we walked to school. "I wonder how long her folks will be gone?"

"I was afraid to ask," Sarah Jane said. "If we don't know for sure, we can pretend that every day is the last one."

The sullen look on Clarice's face when we entered the classroom indicated that she was no happier about the arrangements than we were. She glared at me as I sat down, but she didn't say anything.

"Clarice acts as though I had made her grandmother sick, and on purpose to torment her," I complained to the girls as we walked to our next class. "Why couldn't her mother have hired someone to stay in the house with her?"

"She probably knows what a slippery one Clarice is," Molly ventured. "With three of you watching every move her daughter makes, she won't have to worry about her."

"Count me out," I said. "I'm not playing watchdog for anyone. Can you imagine what my life would be like if I meddled in her affairs?"

We waited by the door after school to walk home with Clarice, but she turned on us angrily.

"What are you standing there for? Do you think it's your responsibility to see that I get home safely?"

"We thought you might want to walk with us," Sarah Jane said.

"You thought wrong. I'm not *that* desperate for company. Just go on about your business." She flounced off, leaving us staring after her in disbelief.

"Well, so much for Be-Nice-to-Clarice Day," Sarah Jane said with a shrug. "I'm going to pretend she isn't there."

We spread our books out on the dining room table where we usually studied and began the next day's lessons. For a couple of hours I forgot about our unwelcome guest as I outlined a history chapter and worked on an English theme. Lettie's voice interrupted my thoughts.

"It's almost time for supper. Where do you suppose Clarice is?"

"I don't know and I don't care," Sarah Jane replied. "She's no concern of mine."

"I *am* responsible for her," Lettie said, "and she's going to have to know that we have rules here. One of them is to be on time when meals are served."

I felt sorry for Lettie. If we acted as bad as Clarice did, Lettie's problems would be tripled.

"I'm sorry, Lettie," I said. "We really haven't had a very good attitude about this. We'll do our best to make Clarice happy while she's here."

"Not me," said Sarah Jane.

"Oh, yes, you will," I told her. "You can't talk about being a Christian unless you act like one. We'll just have to pray for extra patience."

"You're right, Mabel. I should be ashamed of myself. I'll straighten up and do better."

Just as Lettie was about to send Jacob out looking, Clarice stomped into the hallway and slammed the door behind her.

"Where is my room?" she demanded as Lettie met her at the stairway.

"At the end of the hall upstairs," Lettie told her. "And supper will be on the table in five minutes, so come right back down."

Not so much as a hello or how are you? I thought to myself. *What is the matter with that girl?*

Clarice did not reappear, and after we waited for a few minutes, I went to call her. Her door slammed, and she came down the stairs as though she were walking to an execution. When she saw our books on the dining room table, she stopped.

"I thought you said supper was ready," she said. "The table isn't even set."

I pushed open the door to the kitchen. "We eat out here with Lettie and Jacob."

"You don't actually eat with the servants!" she exclaimed.

"No, I eat with my friends. Will you sit down so we can get started?"

Clarice silently took her place, and Jacob asked the blessing. We tried to carry on our usual conversation, but since Clarice would only mutter yes or no when someone spoke to her, it was a difficult meal. When we had finished, Jacob rose to get the Bible. Clarice got up and started for the door.

"We're going to have prayer," Lettie told her. "Where are you going?"

"That's none of your business. I don't have to tell you where I'm going."

Sarah Jane's mouth dropped open, and I gasped in surprise. Jacob put the Bible on the table and spoke in a voice we had never heard before.

"You will not speak to my sister in that tone again as long as you remain in this house, young lady. It *is* our business to know where you are going, and you can be sure we will be minding it. Now sit down while we have family prayer. When we've finished," he added, "you will get your books and tend to your lessons."

The silence that followed this unaccustomed speech was so heavy that we could hear the gentle sizzle of steam from the teakettle on the stove. Jacob adjusted his glasses and opened the Bible.

"Bring your things down and study with us," Sarah Jane suggested as we left the kitchen.

"I'll stay in my room, thank you," Clarice snapped. She marched up the stairs without a backward look.

"Whew!" I said when she was gone. "I thought for a minute Jacob was going to box her ears!"

"If he spoke like that to me, I'd feel as though he had," Sarah Jane replied.

We saw no more of Clarice that night. When we called good night through her closed door, we received only a mumble in return. I went to sleep thinking that the

Lord certainly had his hands full with that one.

Lettie called us at the usual time in the morning, and we heard her rap on Clarice's door.

Sarah Jane rolled over and groaned. "You wouldn't believe the nightmares I had last night," she said. "I dreamed that Clarice burned the house down, and Jacob put beds in the barn for us."

"Well, it's still standing," I replied. "Of course, the day isn't over yet."

When we went down for breakfast, Lettie turned from the stove. "Is Clarice coming?" she asked.

"I didn't hear her moving around," I said. "Maybe she went back to sleep."

"I'll go get her," Sarah Jane offered.

"No," Lettie decided. "She was called, same as you were. She's old enough to get herself out of bed."

We ate breakfast, brushed our teeth, gathered our books, and left for school. There was still no sound from Clarice's room. The first period was almost over when Clarice dashed into class and slid into her seat. She looked furious, and I knew her wrath would descend on me in a short time.

"Why didn't you get me up?" she hissed. "You just wanted to get me into trouble."

"Lettie called you," I reminded her. "We didn't know you needed someone to come in and roll you out of bed."

"Oh, you think you're funny, don't you?" she snapped. "Well, let me tell you something. I'm not going to stay around and let a couple of old servants tell me what to do!"

Clarice was on time for supper, but she still refused to be included in the conversation. As we expected, she retreated to her room immediately afterward.

"This isn't going to be as bad as I expected," Sarah Jane said, as she opened her book. "If we don't have to look at her except during meals, and she doesn't say anything then, we can almost imagine she isn't here."

"That's true," I admitted, "but that's not showing love to our neighbor. She needs to know that we really care about her."

Sarah Jane gazed at me.

"Oh, all right," I said. "So we *don't* really care about her. The point is, we're supposed to. She is a person, you know, and the Lord loves her."

"He's the only one who could," Sarah Jane muttered, and we turned to our lessons.

When we were ready for bed, we again called good night to Clarice through the door. This time there was no sound in reply, not even a cross mumble.

Sarah Jane fell asleep immediately, but I lay looking out the window. I had made no progress toward making Clarice my friend since school began. If anything, she was more hostile toward me than ever. I had prayed about it daily, and I had been careful not to do anything to upset her if I could help it. What else could I do?

It seemed like hours later, when I was about ready to doze off, that I heard a creaking sound in the hallway. My eyes flew open, and I listened intently. The front door opened and closed softly.

"Wake up!" I said, poking Sarah Jane.

"I don't want to," she replied.

"Sarah Jane, please. Wake up. I think Clarice has left the house."

There was silence, and I thought she was still asleep. Then she spoke in a very wide-awake voice.

"Mabel, if the only reason you woke me up was to tell me something I don't care to hear, I'm going to pound you."

"Whether you want to hear it or not, I think Clarice is gone. We've got to do something about it."

Sarah Jane turned over and pounded her pillow. "Good riddance."

"Come *on*!" I insisted. "What shall we do? Should we wake up Lettie?"

"Oh, Mabel," Sarah Jane groaned. "Why do you have to feel so *responsible* for everyone? There's nothing we could do to get her back if we found her. She's dug her own hole. Let her sleep in it."

I could see there would be no help from that direction. I lay back down to ponder what to do next, but before I could reach a decision, I had fallen asleep. A sudden rattle on our window brought us both upright in bed.

"What's that?" Sarah Jane gasped.

"Something hit the window," I replied. "What time is it?"

"How should I know?" Sarah Jane answered crossly. "I've been waked up so many times I'm not even sure what day it is anymore."

We slid out of bed and went to the window. Standing below and looking up at us was Clarice.

Sarah Jane lifted the sash and leaned out. "What in the world are you doing down there?"

"Never mind," Clarice replied. "Just come down and let me in."

"You got out without any help. Why don't you come back the same way?"

"The door locked behind me. Hurry up. It's cold out here."

Sarah Jane closed the window and looked at me. "I don't believe this is happening. It's another nightmare, right?"

"Yes, but unfortunately it's not a sleeping one. And unless we go let her in, there won't be any more sleeping around here."

We went to the top of the stairs, and Sarah Jane ran down to open the door. When they came back up, I pulled Clarice into our room and shut the door.

"What are you doing, anyway? Where have you been?" I demanded.

"It's none of . . . " Clarice began, and then she looked down at the floor. "I don't want to talk about it."

"I don't want to hear about it, either," Sarah Jane told her. "But someone has to be told something. You can't be out running the roads in the middle of the night without—"

The door opened, and Lettie put her head in. "Is someone sick up here?" she said anxiously. Then she spotted Clarice fully dressed.

"Why, Clarice! Haven't you been to bed? It's almost one o'clock!"

"She's—" Sarah Jane started to reply, but I interrupted.

"She had something to say to us," I finished. "She's going to bed right now, aren't you, Clarice?"

Clarice nodded and left for her room. Lettie looked confused, told us good night, and went back downstairs.

"Why did you cover for her?" Sarah Jane demanded. "She needs to be punished! I think Lettie ought to know what she's doing."

"I thought maybe if she knew we weren't going to tell on her, she'd let us help her," I said.

"Hah!" Sarah Jane answered. "You know better than that. She hasn't any use for us or anyone else, that I know of."

We climbed back into bed.

"Sarah Jane, how do you suppose we would have turned out if we'd had Mrs. Owens for a mother?"

There was no answer, but I knew Sarah Jane was thinking it over.

12
Hearts And Arrows

FEBRUARY 12, 1890. We've no idea how much longer we'll have to put up with Clarice, but even one more day will seem like forever. Lettie doesn't say much, but she has fire in her eye.

CLARICE WAS ON TIME FOR BREAKFAST the next morning. If we thought she would be chastened after the previous evening's experience, we were due for a disappointment. We started out for school together, but we were barely out of sight of the house before Clarice turned on me angrily.

"I suppose you think I should be grateful to you for not telling Lettie I was out last night," she stormed. "Well, you don't have to feel so self-righteous. I don't care whether you tell her or not. She isn't in charge of me."

"Why didn't you tell her yourself, then?" Sarah Jane spoke up. "And there's nothing self-righteous about Mabel. She covered for you because she has a good heart!"

Clarice sniffed and stalked off down the road ahead of us. I, for one, was ready to let her go.

"I wish I knew what I had done to her," I said. "At first I thought she was just making fun of me because I came from the country, but now I think she really hates me."

"I'm beginning to think you're right," Sarah Jane agreed. "It's more than just a nasty disposition."

At noon we tried to dismiss the problem from our minds as we talked with Molly.

"Lettie said we could have some friends over Friday evening for a valentine party," I told her. "Whom shall we ask?"

"Well, there will be the three of us, and Warren, Russ, and Thomas. Let's ask Matilda, and she can bring a friend. That's eight. Who else?"

"Clarice will probably still be there," Sarah Jane reminded us. "She'll have to invite someone, too. I suppose it will be that horrid Victor Linden."

We pondered this silently for a moment. "What can we do about it?" I said. "You can't tell a houseguest to stay in her room because you don't want her at your party."

"You could invite someone for her," Molly suggested. "Ask whomever you want to be her partner. After all, it's your party."

This seemed like an excellent idea, so after much discussion, we settled on Melvin Wells as the extra boy.

"It's not as though we were pairing off in couples exactly," Sarah Jane pointed out. "Matilda and Molly are the only ones who will have to be called for. The other boys can come together."

We almost succeeded in forgetting about Clarice in our excitement over planning games and inviting the others.

"What do you want for refreshments Friday evening?" Lettie asked us at suppertime. "And how many will be here?"

Clarice looked up from her plate, and I blushed to realize that we hadn't even spoken to her about the party.

"There will be ten, Lettie," I answered. Then I told Clarice who would be coming.

"How nice of you to invite someone for me," she said sarcastically. "At least I won't embarrass you with my choice of friends. I'm sure I wouldn't be included either, if I weren't already here."

This was true, and neither of us had an answer. Jacob ended the awkward silence with an offer we were happy to accept.

"Maybe you'd like to have a sleigh ride to start the evening out," he said. "Weather's just about perfect for it."

We attempted to draw Clarice into preparations for the party. "We're going to cut out five hearts," Sarah Jane explained. "We'll cut each one in two with a jagged line. The boys will pick half a heart and the girls the other half. The one whose half matches yours will be your partner for the evening. Do you want to help us make them, Clarice?"

She grudgingly consented to assist us, so Sarah Jane drew them, I cut them out, and Clarice divided them. They were placed in separate boxes to be drawn later.

"What games shall we play when we get back?" I asked. "Do you know some, Clarice?"

"Games are pretty childish, but I might be able to think of something that wouldn't bore everyone," she replied. "I'll be in charge of them if you want me to."

"That scares me silly," Sarah Jane confided as we got ready for bed. "Who knows what she'll come up with?"

"Certainly she knows that there are some things Christians wouldn't do," I said. "It's a step in the right direction just to have her showing interest."

But I couldn't help feeling a bit apprehensive, and I prayed that the Lord would keep Clarice from ruining our party.

On Valentine Day she seemed almost

cheerful. I didn't consider that a good omen.

"She's up to something," Sarah Jane said darkly after Clarice smiled at her on the way down to breakfast. Remembering the glares we had endured all week, it seemed highly probable.

"What can she do besides suggest games no one wants to play?" I said. "The sleigh ride and eating will take most of the evening, anyway. And who knows? Maybe her folks will get home today and she won't even stay for the party."

"You *are* a dreamer," Sarah Jane said. "She'd never miss a chance to be the center of attention."

So even though I had thought of it, we weren't prepared for Clarice's announcement at noon.

"My parents are home," she said, "so I won't be going back to your house after school. They've already gotten my things. I'm sure you're not going to miss me, are you?"

Before I could speak, she continued.

"I'll still come to the party, since you so graciously included me. I asked Russ if he'd come and get me. I didn't think you'd mind."

She could have punched me in the stomach and the effect would have been no different. For once even Sarah Jane was speechless. I sat through my afternoon classes, but not much information entered my head. Molly walked home with us after school.

"There's no point in asking what you're going to do, Mabel," she said. "You'll just turn the other cheek and give her your coat. How could she do that?"

"I don't own Russ," I said. "He's free to go with anyone he wants to."

"Oh, stop being so reasonable!" Sarah Jane snapped. "Russ hasn't asked another girl out all school year. You know he'd rather be with you."

"He could have said so," Molly put in. "He didn't have to bring her just because she asked him."

"He's too much of a gentleman to just say no," I said. "After all, we hadn't made any other arrangements than just everyone coming. Maybe I'll get the other half of his heart."

It was dark by six-thirty. Jacob had the sleigh ready, piled with hay and heavy carriage blankets. The pair of horses stamped the ground, and the bells on their harnesses sang out in the cold air. It had begun to snow softly.

"All the ingredients for a perfect party," Lettie said as we waited for the others to arrive. "You'll have a lovely time tonight. Do you have your hearts all ready to hand out?"

I nodded. Everything did look perfect, but I wasn't really happy. I resented Clarice asking my boyfriend, though I hadn't thought of him that way before, to escort her. My only hope lay in the boxes of paper hearts.

"Everyone is here except Russ and Clarice," Sarah Jane announced. "Let's go ahead and draw our hearts. They can get theirs when they arrive."

When the matching was complete, I sighed with relief. Mine didn't fit anyone's, and neither did Warren's. That meant that Clarice and Russ would have the two left over. She wouldn't have a complete victory anyway.

We were all settled in the sleigh when they arrived.

"Are you all ready to go?" Clarice said brightly. "Since everyone has a partner, I'll just keep the one I have. That will be fine, won't it, Russ? Can you help me up in the sleigh?"

Russ lifted her in and climbed up himself. He looked at me with a puzzled expression, but I turned away. If that was the kind of girl he wanted, let him have her.

I suppose the ride was great fun. Everyone sang and laughed and talked happily. It all whirled around in my head, but I was only conscious of one thing. I despised Clarice Owens.

By the time we returned home we could only play one game before Lettie had the food ready. Sandwiches, hot chocolate, and valentine tarts were on the big table. Jacob had polished apples and popped corn. We filled our plates and chose places to sit with our partners.

The food looked delicious, but I wasn't hungry. Warren ate steadily and talked about the party. "This has sure been a lot of fun," he said. "We need something like this every month."

I kept quiet.

"Say, Mabel," Warren continued, "are you put out with Russ about something?"

"Now why would you think that?"

"Oh, I don't know," Warren answered. "He just wondered why you sent word with Clarice that he was to bring her to the party instead of you."

"I sent what?" I yelped. "He said I did that?"

"Well, *she* said you did. Is something wrong, Mabel?"

I jumped up to corner Clarice, but she saw me coming and quickly turned her back. In the process, her cup of chocolate poured down the front of my skirt.

"Oh, how awful!" Clarice said. "But you were right in the way, Mabel."

The look on her face was more than I could take, and I faced her furiously, ready to give her the full benefit of my wrath. In the sudden silence, I realized that everyone was listening, and I swallowed my angry words.

"Excuse me. I'll go and change my skirt."

As I ran up the stairs, I could hear Clarice's laughter and the voices of the others as the party continued. I took off my skirt and sat down on the end of my bed. *I have never been so furious in my whole life*, I thought. I wanted to scream, but I knew that wouldn't do, with all those people in the house. Instead, I clamped my teeth into the poster of the bed. When I had calmed down, I went back to the party. Sarah Jane and Molly looked at me anxiously, but there was no opportunity to talk.

After everyone had left, we helped Lettie pick up in the front room and dining room, and then went up to bed.

"Mabel, how in the world did you keep from hitting that horrid girl? I would have flattened her!"

"I almost did," I replied. "But she was a guest here. You can't go knocking your guests around."

I turned to the mirror to brush my hair.

"Mabel," Sarah Jane's voice sounded odd. "What happened to this bed?"

"I bit it."

"You *bit* it? You actually bit the *bed*?" Sarah Jane collapsed on the end of it and shrieked with laughter. As mad as I was, I had to join her.

"Well, I couldn't very well bite Clarice, could I?" I said when she had subsided. "But I'll tell you one thing. I'm going to find out what's the matter with that girl if it's the last thing I do."

13
Mrs. Owens
Has Her Say

MARCH 5, 1890. I wrote to Ma about my problems with Clarice. She says I must continue to pray for her and treat her as a friend. But how do you be a friend to someone who stabs you in the back? I'm glad both Ma and Pa are praying for me.

I ROLLED OVER IN BED AND LOOKED AT the sunshine coming in the window. It was going to be a beautiful spring day.

"I just love Saturdays," I said to Sarah Jane. "We can sleep in—"

"So why don't you?" she mumbled into her pillow.

"It's almost eight o'clock," I replied. "I can hear Jacob getting water from the rain barrel for our hair. And I can smell Lettie's good doughnuts."

She sat up. "Umm. Now that you mention it, so can I."

We quickly dressed and stripped the bed. Lettie would bring up clean sheets after breakfast.

Sarah Jane paused to glance out the window. "I think it looks warm enough to dry our hair outside, if we stay out of the wind and in the sun. Don't you think so?"

I nodded. "In fact, I may stay out in the sun all day long. You'll have to bring me my dinner at noon."

Lettie laughed when we told her. "I'm afraid it's a little early for that. It looks warm, but you'll find the air is pretty cool. This is fickle weather. It may be snowing by tonight."

I started to protest, till I thought of another spring day that had started out warm and balmy.

"Sarah Jane, do you remember the day we cut the legs off our long underwear, and then got caught in a blizzard?"

"How could I forget it?" she replied. "Ma sewed mine back together, and I had to wear them like that until I outgrew them."

"Are the boys coming over this evening?" Lettie asked as we dried our hair.

"Yes," Sarah Jane answered, "and Warren and Molly, too. Thomas has a new game he wants us to play. I'm certainly glad you straightened things out with Russ," she said to me. "I thought for a while you weren't going to tell him that it wasn't your idea that he bring Clarice to the valentine party."

"I might not have," I said, "but he asked me. I think he suspected it might have been all Clarice's doing."

Jacob was sitting on the porch, mending a chair. We heard him chuckle.

"Things don't change much over the years."

"They tend to get older," Lettie replied. "What else did you have in mind?"

"I was thinking of the Bradley boy and the Owens girl," he replied. "When I remember what happened back when we were in school, it appears to me that the valentine business may not have been *all* Clarice's idea."

"Now, Jacob, how you talk. Although you may be right. Gertrude hasn't changed a great deal."

"Did you go to school with Mrs. Owens?" Sarah Jane wanted to know.

"Oh, yes," Jacob answered. "And Russ Bradley's folks, too. Gertrude was determined to have John Bradley, but he chose Martha Russell instead. I don't think Gertrude ever got over it."

"Do you suppose Mrs. Owens is just as determined that Clarice will have Russ?" Sarah Jane wondered.

"Wouldn't be surprised," Lettie said. "And Gertrude is a strong-willed woman."

Sarah Jane looked at me thoughtfully.

"That explains some of it, Mabel. Clarice has been unhappy because you've been more popular than she has almost since school started. On top of that, she probably thinks Russ belongs to her by reason of inheritance, and you came in and took him away from her."

"That's no answer," I protested. "That's another complication. And even if it's true, what can I do about it? Parents don't choose husbands for their daughters anymore."

"I wouldn't count on it," Jacob said drily, "especially when you consider who the parent is."

While we were getting ready for supper, I voiced my thoughts to Sarah Jane.

"You never know when you're bringing trouble on your head, do you? Here I thought Clarice was to blame, and I'm causing it myself, by being friends with Russ."

Sarah Jane stared at me in disbelief. "Mabel O'Dell, that is the most ridiculous thing I've ever heard you say—and that's saying something. What could you do about it? Tell Russ, 'Sorry, but I can't keep company with you because Mrs. Owens wants you to marry her daughter'? He'd think you were out of your mind! And he'd be right."

"The Bible says, 'as much as lieth in *you,* keep peace with all men.' Letting Clarice have Russ is something I could do," I replied.

Now Sarah Jane was really annoyed. "Who gave you the right to hand Russ around like a piece of pie? Did it ever occur to you that he might like you better than he does Clarice?"

"I hadn't thought about that," I said meekly.

"Well, think about it," she snapped. "If you try to run Russ's life by telling him he should pay attention to Clarice, you're as bad as Mrs. Owens is."

"I guess you're right," I admitted.

"Let's forget about Clarice and have fun this evening," Sarah Jane suggested. "The others will be here right after supper."

The Parcheesi game Thomas brought was such fun that neither of us gave Clarice another thought.

Lettie brought us cookies and apples to eat. "Jacob and I have to go into town to pick up a few things," she told us. "We'll be back in about half an hour. If you want more to eat, you know where to find it."

"Thanks, Lettie," Sarah Jane said. "When you get back, you and Jacob should come and play with us."

"That was the most fun I've had in a long time," I said as we were getting ready for bed. "We need to do this more often."

Lettie was right about the spring weather not staying. There was snow on the ground when we awoke Sunday morning.

"It may melt off before evening," Jacob predicted. "This is good sugaring weather. Snappy nights and sunny days."

"We'll be ready for church in just a few minutes," Lettie said after breakfast. "You'll need your scarves and gloves again."

We arrived at church early enough to greet Russ and Thomas before the service began.

"How about going for a walk this afternoon?" Thomas said. "We can go right after dinner and be back in time for young people's meeting."

"That will be fun," Sarah Jane agreed. "We'll see you then."

The boys left to sit with their families, and Sarah Jane and I joined Jacob and Lettie. From the pew where she sat with her parents, Clarice turned to look at us. I recognized the expression that meant there was nothing good in store for us.

"Now what?" I whispered to Sarah Jane. "Something tells me she's ready to spring another trap."

Sarah Jane nodded. "Let's stay away from her."

We followed Jacob and Lettie out when

church was over and arrived at the door in time to hear Mrs. Owens speaking to Rev. Charles.

"You know I don't like to carry tales or cause trouble," she said, "but I think you ought to know what is going on. After all, you are the shepherd of this flock."

"Yes, Mrs. Owens," Reverend Charles sighed. "What is it?"

"It's come to my attention," Mrs. Owens replied with evident satisfaction, "that some of the young people of this congregation are spending their evenings together playing useless games. I think it is your duty, since one of the young persons is your own son, to stop this wasteful practice. We all know that activities which do not benefit the soul can be tools of the Devil. Of course, recreation once in a while is not all bad, but this could become a habit."

She waited a moment to see how this piece of news would affect the minister. Since he said nothing, she went on.

"I also know for a fact that while this game playing was going on, those same young people were left alone and unchaperoned in the house!"

She looked around at us triumphantly.

"I'm sure you see where your Christian responsibility lies, Rev. Charles. I certainly would never allow *my* daughter's reputation to be sullied by such associations. Now understand, I'm not blaming your son as much as I do certain first-year students." She glared in our direction again. "I've done what I felt I should do as a Christian. Now it's up to you to take action."

Mrs. Owens descended the stairs with the feathers on her hat bobbing indignantly, the very picture of righteousness on the march.

Clarice sidled past with a parting remark. "You're in trouble now!"

To say that we were dumbfounded would be an understatement. I felt as though I were glued to the spot. Lettie's cheeks were red, and Jacob's eyebrows came together over his eyes, but they both shook hands calmly with the minister. We followed them numbly to the buggy to go home.

"That miserable old busybody has gone too far this time," Jacob muttered. "I've a notion to go over there and give her a good tongue-lashing!"

"Least said, soonest mended," Lettie reminded him. "When you haven't done anything wrong, there's no need to defend yourself."

"We weren't unchaperoned!" cried Sarah Jane. "You were both there with us!"

"We were gone for half an hour," Lettie

reminded her. "I suppose she or Clarice saw us in town. Rev. Charles is a sensible person and a man of God. I'm sure he'll take into consideration the source of the complaint."

We trusted Lettie's judgment, but I was feeling worse by the moment.

"Now there are six of us in trouble because Clarice hates me," I said. "Where is it all going to stop? I'd almost rather just back off and let her have her own way."

"Oh, no, you don't!" Sarah Jane declared. "You're not going to budge an inch. You said yourself that the Lord would fight our battles for us if we do what's right. And you've done what's right."

"That's easy for you to say," I retorted. "I think this whole business is going to make me old before my time."

"Father said not to worry about Mrs. Owens," Thomas informed us as we headed toward the woods on our walk. "He'll tell her that he talked to me about it, and it's taken care of. That's just one of the hazards of being a preacher's son."

I looked at him in surprise. "Do you think *you're* the one Mrs. Owens has it in for?"

"Why, yes. Who else would it be? Don't you remember the fuss on Halloween night? I missed the whole party because she complained to Father."

"I think you're both taking Mrs. Owens's spitefulness too personally," Sarah Jane said. "You have to give her credit for one thing: she treats everyone to the same ornery disposition."

We decided that Sarah Jane was right and went on to talk of other things. But when I prayed that night, I didn't ask the Lord to bless Clarice. Neither did I ask him to get rid of her exactly, although I suggested that some distance between us wouldn't hurt my feelings.

As I was drifting off to sleep, I remembered Ma saying that we shouldn't expect the Lord to nag our enemies for us—all he knows how to do is love them.

14

The Most Important Event

MARCH 28, 1890. There are a lot of spring activities going on now. The most important will be the annual speech contest sponsored by the Aradelphians. I can hardly wait to try out for it. I'm sure I can qualify.

ENGLISH CLASS WAS OVER, AND I walked from the room in a daze.

"Mabel," I heard Sarah Jane call, "where are you going?"

"My next class," I replied.

"You won't get there going that way," she said. "Come on." She took my arm and turned me around in the hallway.

"She's trying to drive me crazy, isn't she?" I asked Molly. "She wants me to lose my mind. Is that why she did that?"

"Certainly not," Molly replied. "Clarice never does anything that doesn't lead eventually to her advantage. I think she told you the truth."

I thought over the previous hour's events, beginning with Miss Baker's announcement.

"Class, our assignment today will be a continuing one. On the 25th of next month the spring program is scheduled. It will consist of speeches, declamations, readings, and dialogues. We will begin by preparing dialogues. You will each have a partner to work with, and the team with the best presentation will represent the class in the program. Next week, we'll all work on readings and choose the best. Are there any questions?"

Clarice raised her hand. "Miss Baker, I'd like to volunteer to work with Mabel on the dialogue."

All eyes turned in her direction, and my mouth dropped open in amazement. She smiled sweetly at me.

"That will be fine, Clarice," Miss Baker answered. "Now, how about the rest of you?"

"How come?" I demanded of Clarice when we met with our partners. "You can't stand the sight of me!"

"That's true," Clarice agreed, "but I think you have a chance at first place. I like to be on a winning team."

"If she thinks I'm going to get a good grade for both of us, I have news for her," I told Sarah Jane. "She's going to have to do her share of the work."

"Clarice is a good student," Sarah Jane

admitted grudgingly. "She's also a good speaker. You've heard her."

So what did she need me for? I was sure she had some plot for my downfall, but what could it be? A dialogue required the cooperation of two people, and that was the last thing I had come to expect from Clarice.

After school we chose our material from books offered by Miss Baker. "A dialogue from *Alice in Wonderland* would be fun," she suggested. "Look at the one with the Mock Turtle."

Clarice and I read a bit of it together.

Mock Turtle: *When we were little, we went to school in the sea. The master was an old turtle; we used to call him Tortoise—*

Alice: *Why did you call him Tortoise if he wasn't one?*

Mock Turtle: *We called him Tortoise because he taught us! Really, you are very dull. We had the best of education; in fact, we went to school every day—*

Alice: *I've been to a day school, too. You needn't be so proud as all that!*

Mock Turtle: (anxiously) *With extras?*

Alice: *Yes. We learned French and music.*

Mock Turtle: *And washing?*

Alice: (indignantly) *Certainly not!*

Mock Turtle: (with great relief) *Ah! Then yours wasn't a really good school. Now at* ours, *they had at the end of the bill, "French, music, and* washing, *extra!"*

"Oh, I like this!" Clarice exclaimed. "We can even end it by singing a verse of 'Beautiful Soup.' Would you rather be Mock Turtle or Alice?"

"Why don't we both learn both parts, and then decide?" I suggested.

Clarice agreed, and I took a copy home to begin learning it.

"Mabel, are you memorizing that?" Sarah Jane's voice broke in on my thoughts.

"What? Yes, of course. What do you think I'm doing?"

"You're still wondering what Clarice is up to. I can tell by the glazed look in your eye."

"Well, wouldn't you be?" I asked. "When has she ever directed anything good or helpful or kind toward me? What would *you* be thinking?"

"It is most unusual. But you'll still have to do your best on your part."

"I intend to," I retorted. "I intend to do better than my best. But I'm not going to stop watching for whatever she has in mind."

We practiced each afternoon when classes were over. As the days went by, I had to admit that Clarice was doing an excellent job. I was even forced to acknowledge that she was a better speaker than I was.

"She hasn't even made any disparaging remarks," I said to the girls. "I know I'm awful to be so suspicious, but I just can't help it. What could have brought this on?"

"Clarice likes to be a winner," Molly said. "And she's smart enough to know if you can't beat 'em, you join 'em."

"I suppose so," I sighed. "It's just that I don't trust her as far as I can see her. Goodness knows I haven't had much reason to!"

On Friday Mr. Kingman came to English class to help judge the dialogues. The other members of the class were also given a vote. Clarice and I won unanimously, and her eyes sparkled as we sat down.

"We'll be in the spring program," she said. "It will be a real honor. I suppose I should thank you for that."

"Don't bother," I replied. "Neither one of us could have done it alone."

"I guess this proves you can work together toward a common goal, no matter what you think of another person," I said to Sarah Jane later. "If this keeps up, I may be forced to revise my opinion of Clarice Owens."

"Don't be too hasty," she advised me. "She's not doing it just to make *you* look good. She's right about it being an honor. The whole town turns out for this program."

While the class went on to choose the speakers in the other divisions, we were excused to polish our part. We worked hard and were satisfied with our efforts.

"If this could have happened at the beginning of the year, I might actually have liked Clarice," I confided to Lettie. "She can be really decent when she wants to be."

"Everyone has a good side if you can find it," Lettie said. "Sometimes they don't even know it themselves."

"I don't think being on the program, even if your dialogue is the best part of it, is going to make up for her losing Russ," Sarah Jane said. "I can't see her letting that matter go without a struggle."

"She has as much chance as I have," I shrugged. "He's free to choose whichever one he wants."

"I thought you liked Russ."

"I do," I replied. "I like him a lot. But I don't have any claim on him. I guess I would be disappointed if he decided to go with someone else, though."

"I don't think there's much chance," Sarah Jane laughed. "He hasn't seen anyone but you since the first program of the year."

Having to spend a lot of time with Clarice, I found that she was more clever and witty than I had imagined. In fact, when she wasn't sniping at me, I actually enjoyed talking with her.

"This spring program is the biggest event of the year in town," she told me one afternoon. "I've never been in one before. It draws as big a crowd as the Chautauqua."

"I hope we don't get nervous and forget everything we learned," I said. "That could be embarrassing."

Clarice shook her head. "We won't do that. We've gone over it so often we could say it in our sleep. Anyway, aren't you the one who has the Lord on your side?"

"That's not a guarantee that everything I do is going to win a blue ribbon," I told her. "The Lord expects me to do the hard work."

As the day approached for the program, it became harder for me to concentrate on my studies. I wasn't worried about our dialogue, but the excitement of the big event seemed to carry over into the rest of our days.

"I'll be glad when you get back to normal," Molly said. "I couldn't believe that Latin translation you did this morning."

"It was a simple mistake," I said defensively. "Could I help it if I turned two pages at once?"

"Couldn't you tell from what the person ahead of you read that you were in the wrong place?" Sarah Jane wanted to know.

"I didn't even hear what he read," I admitted. "I was thinking about something else."

"I guess so. I hope you come back safely to earth when this program is over."

Friday the 25th finally arrived. We had shortened classes so that most of the afternoon would be free, but I could see that the day couldn't possibly go fast enough for me.

"Whatever you're planning to wear tonight is going to fall off you if you don't eat more than you have this past week," Lettie scolded at breakfast time. "Why is it that every time you get upset or excited you take it out on your food?"

"I don't know," I replied. "It's just that my stomach gets jumpy. I'll try to eat."

Everyone was milling about the room and talking when we arrived in our first class.

Miss Baker was understanding. "Let's sit down, class, and compose ourselves. I know this is a big day, but it won't go any faster by being disorganized. We'll use this period for free reading or study. Do what you like, but do it quietly."

It was several moments later when I noticed that the seat behind me was empty. "Where's Clarice?" I whispered to Molly. "Did she decide school would be too much to stand today?"

"Oh, dear," Molly replied. "She's sick. I

didn't want to be the one to tell you."

"Sick? You mean *sick in bed* sick?"

Molly nodded. "Papa had to go see her last night. Mrs. Owens thought it might be nerves, but Papa says she has a fever."

"She'll be well by evening, won't she?" I asked. "She won't have to miss the program?"

"I don't know," Molly replied. "I hope she'll be all right."

Gradually the truth began to sink in. Without Clarice, our part of the program would have to be canceled. I was not going to appear in the biggest event of the year.

"Maybe something can be done," Sarah Jane suggested as we talked it over after class. "Miss Baker will think of something."

"Like what?" I said bitterly. "This is a dialogue, Sarah Jane. I can't get up there and talk to myself."

"Isn't there someone else who knows Clarice's part, or could learn it by tonight?" Molly wondered. "No, I guess not," she added, seeing the look on my face.

"She's done this on purpose," I stormed. "I knew I shouldn't be getting so complacent about that girl. She's tried every way she can think of to make me look bad, but this time she's gone too far!"

"Be sensible, Mabel," Sarah Jane said.

"This was just as important to Clarice as it was to you. I don't think she'd deliberately ruin your chances."

"Whose side are you on, anyway?" I interrupted her. "I never thought I'd hear you stand up for Clarice against me!" I stomped angrily off toward biology class, leaving a stricken-looking Sarah Jane to walk by herself.

By the time school was dismissed at noon, I had decided that I would confront Clarice. I had been patient with her long enough.

I hurried angrily toward the Owenses' house, and every step I took reminded me of something Clarice had done or said to make me look bad. The list was long and included injuries suffered from the first day of school right up to the present. I intended to tell her everything I had been thinking all year long.

Suddenly a thought occurred to me, and I slowed my steps. Hadn't I told the Lord that I would forgive Clarice and return good for evil? What kind of Christian was I if I could tolerate her only when she was friendly and behaved the way I wanted her to? I was ashamed of my anger, and turned around to start back home.

No, I decided, *I'll go see her and tell her I'm sorry she has to miss the program. At least I'll be there to enjoy it, even if I can't take part.*

Mrs. Owens met me at the door. "Oh, it's you," she said. "I didn't expect to see you around here."

"I'd like to see Clarice, Mrs. Owens," I replied. "Will it be all right?"

"I suppose so. Just don't get her upset."

Clarice heard me come in, but she didn't turn to look at me. "I know why you're here," she said. "You came to yell at me for ruining our chances for first place. You think I did it on purpose."

"No," I replied. "I'll admit I was ready to yell when I saw you weren't in school this morning, but now I'm here to tell you I'm sorry you're sick. I know you were as anxious about this program as I was. I'm really sorry."

She turned her head to face me. "Mabel, I've treated you like dirt all year long, because I was jealous of you. I thought if I could make you mad enough to do something terrible, your friends wouldn't like you so much. But you always surprise me by forgiving me or acting as though it didn't happen. How come you've never been mean to me?"

"I've been taught that it's better to love than to hate," I replied. "It isn't always easier, but I've discovered that hating makes *me* feel worse. I'd rather be your friend than your enemy, Clarice."

Her eyes filled with tears, and she brushed them away impatiently. "All right," she said, "you win. You can't go on disliking someone who refuses to be disliked. And I really feel terrible about tonight."

"I know," I said, "but we'll have another chance next year. I'll come by tomorrow and tell you all about the program, shall I?"

She nodded, and I left to find Sarah Jane and Molly. My heart felt lighter than it had for many months, and I had to share the news with my friends.

15
A Friend
Is Forever

MAY 31, 1890. The school year is almost over, and we'll be going home for the summer. S.J.'s aunt and uncle have written to say that we must come back next year so they can enjoy having us here! I can't think of anything that would make us want to miss our last year. The Lord has been good to give us such an opportunity.

"TWO MORE WEEKS," SARAH JANE announced as we slid into our places at breakfast. "One week of classes and one week of exams, then graduation."

"Next year at this time *you'll* be graduating," Lettie said. "How the days fly by!"

"That's a whole year away, Lettie," I said. "It seems like forever to me."

"It won't when you're my age," she replied, "but I'm glad you think so. I'm looking forward to your coming again in the fall."

"So are we," I told her. "A summer at home looks pretty good, but I know I'll be glad to get back to school."

"Isn't this the day of the honor assembly?" Jacob asked.

I nodded. "We have half a day of classes and then we go back at two o'clock for the assembly. That means we'll be home for dinner this noon."

Lettie looked dismayed. "Oh, dear, I forgot all about that! Jacob and I have some business to take care of, and we won't be back until the middle of the afternoon."

"Don't worry about us, Lettie," Sarah Jane said. "We can get our own dinner."

Lettie was relieved. "We'll be back in plenty of time for supper. I'm putting a pot of beans in the oven this morning. Since you'll be here, would you mind taking them out before you leave for the assembly? Just put them at the back of the stove to stay warm."

"Sure," I said. "We'll do that."

"You'd better let me remember it," Sarah Jane told me. "I'd just as soon not have burned beans tonight."

Before I could reply, Jacob asked about the awards. "How many are you two getting?"

"We're each getting a scholastic award," I answered, "and I'm getting one for speech."

"And I'll receive a perfect attendance certificate," Sarah Jane added. "I haven't been tardy or missed a class all year."

"That's a good record," Lettie said. "If it

hadn't been for Mabel's accident, she'd have had one, too."

"You're going to lose that one today if we don't get started," I said. "Look what time it is!"

We grabbed our books and rushed out the door. "Why were you so slow this morning?" Sarah Jane said. "We didn't even get to have prayer before we left. Now we'll be rushed all day long."

"Jacob will pray for us," I said. "And I wasn't any slower than you were. Who had to go back upstairs to get her notebook?"

"Don't act so superior, Mabel," Sarah Jane said crossly. "You forget ten things while I'm forgetting one. You're the person with your head in the clouds and your nose in a book."

We arrived in our classroom just seconds before the bell rang.

"I can't believe the luxury of having two hours for noon recess," Molly said as we walked to our second period class. "Why don't you come home with me for dinner?"

"We could do that," Sarah Jane said. "Lettie and Jacob are gone, and we were going to have to get our own."

"That would be fun," I agreed. "Are your folks coming for the assembly?"

"Mama will," Molly replied, "but Papa has office hours." She gave a sigh. "I hope he can get away from his patients long enough to come and see me graduate next year."

"Don't worry," I said, "he wouldn't miss that. I guess there's an advantage to being a farmer's daughter. Pa never missed anything at school that we had a part in."

I had a sudden twinge of longing for my home and the familiar faces of Ma and Pa. At that moment two weeks seemed longer than the rest of the year had been.

History class turned into a study period, since Mr. Kingman was busy preparing for the assembly.

"It's too bad you won't have anyone here to see you get your awards," Clarice said to me. "You've certainly worked hard for them."

"They'll be thinking about me," I replied, "and they'll see them when I get home."

The biggest award I have is a truce with you, I added silently. *That's worth more than all the rest put together.*

Mrs. Matson welcomed us at dinnertime. "We'll miss you girls this summer," she said. "Molly has been happier this year than she's ever been in school."

"We were hoping Molly could come and spend some time with us this summer," Sarah Jane said. "Do you think she could?"

"I don't see why not, if your parents won't mind," Mrs. Matson replied. "Maybe that will help her live through the vacation."

We finished dinner and went to sit on the porch until time to go back to school. While the girls were talking, I thought about the beans in the oven at home. I opened my mouth to remind Sarah Jane, but then thought again. *She was so uppity about my forgetting,* I thought, *I'll wait and see how good her memory is.*

At just that moment the boys came around the house. "We thought we'd find you here," Thomas said. "Are you all ready to pick up your honors?"

Warren chimed in. "Too bad you couldn't quite 'add' the math award to your list, Mabel. But never mind—you'll probably only have to teach the first eight grades."

"Warren," I said, "if I hadn't known you since we were born, I'd probably dislike you intensely."

"I'm just teasing," he replied. "Actually, Mabel, you have a pretty good brain—for a girl."

I glared at him, and Russ laughed. "You'd better back off, Warren. You're going to be chewing shoe leather in a minute."

Mrs. Matson came to the door. "It's about time for you to get started," she said. "Are you going directly to the assembly?"

"We have to report to our study room and

go with the class," Molly answered. "But you get there early so you'll have a good seat."

We strolled back to school, enjoying the lovely spring day. Shortly after two o'clock, we were dismissed to go to the assembly room. Molly and I walked together.

"Where's Sarah Jane?" I wondered.

"She went out ahead of us," Molly said. "She's probably saving us a seat."

The room seemed full of visitors when we entered, and I looked around to see whom I might know. Near the back I spied Jacob and Lettie.

"Oh, look, Molly!" I said. "They came to be our family. Wasn't that sweet?"

Molly hurried me toward the front where the students were sitting. We couldn't see Sarah Jane anywhere, so we found two vacant places and sat down. The program was just ready to begin when things clicked together in my brain.

"Oh, no!" I cried. "The beans!"

People around looked at me strangely as I started to get up. Molly pulled me down.

"You can't leave now," she whispered. "Mr. Kingman is starting to speak."

I sank into my seat with a moan. Why hadn't I reminded Sarah Jane when I thought of it? This time my stubbornness was going to affect everyone. Supper would

be ruined and Sarah Jane would feel awful.
I'd have to tell her how sorry I was, but that
wouldn't save the beans.

Through my tumbled thoughts I heard Mr.
Kingman calling people's names and saw
them go forward. Then he said, "Now we
come to a most important certificate. We
place great emphasis on steady attendance
and punctuality. I'm always pleased when
we have a group of students who have
maintained a perfect record. Will these pu-
pils please come for their award? Katherine
Borden . . ."

"Now we'll see where she's sitting," Molly
whispered. "She's next."

"Sarah Jane Clark," Mr. Kingman said.

There was silence.

"Sarah Jane?" Mr. Kingman peered
around the room. "She wouldn't be absent
when she was about to get a perfect attendance award, would she?"

People snickered and looked around. I
grabbed Molly's arm frantically. "Where is
she? Didn't you see her leave the room?"

"Yes, and I thought she was coming here.
Where could she have gone?"

I was beginning to think I knew, and I felt
worse than ever. She had suddenly remembered the beans in the oven and had gone
home to take them out.

Mr. Kingman was going on with the list. When he had finished, he looked around the room again.

"Is Sarah Jane Clark here now?" he asked.

"Yes, sir," came a voice from the doorway, and Sarah Jane hurried down the aisle. Her face was flushed, her usually neat hair was hanging in little wisps around her face, and she was breathing heavily.

"I'm sure whatever kept you was unavoidable," Mr. Kingman said kindly. "Here is your certificate." He shook her hand, and Sarah Jane sat down on the other side of the room!"

"Oh, I could just die!" I said. "To think I'd do a thing like that to my best friend!"

"What did *you* do?" Molly asked in bewilderment. "And where has she been? What's this all about?"

"I'll tell you later," I said. "That is, if I live long enough."

The assembly didn't last a lot longer, but I could have waited the rest of the afternoon before having to face Sarah Jane. We found her waiting in the hallway when we were dismissed.

"I always say that if you're going to make a spectacle of yourself, be sure you have a good audience," she announced cheerfully. "I ran all the way home and all the way back in just under ten minutes. And I'll never say anything about your memory again, Mabel. If I hadn't seen Lettie when I walked in here, I'd never have thought of those beans the rest of the day."

"I'm glad you girls are so good-natured," Jacob said when we told them what had happened. "I'd hate to see a pot of beans break up a friendship like yours."

"Never," Sarah Jane said. "We've gone through a lot of outrageous things together, but none of them has ever changed the way we feel about each other. I've never lived without Mabel. Would you want me to start now? After all—a friend is forever!"

Jacob and Lettie laughed and agreed. And I quietly thanked the Lord for a good friend like Sarah Jane. She was right. Life would not be the same without her.